CONTENTS

Preface

The purpose of this book is to introduce foreign residents in Japan to the pleasures of Japanese home cooking. Many people believe Japanese cuisine is beyond them, but in actual fact it is quite simple.

The dishes introduced herein were chosen because they are healthful, economical and quick to prepare. They are recipes that have been handed down from generation to generation and are still the bill of fare in Japanese homes today.

A typical family meal comprises soup, three main dishes — something raw, fried and grilled — served with rice and pickles. Or a variation thereof. As well as traditional foods Japanese enjoy cuisine of other cultures; often some of these dishes are adapted to local tastes and incorporated as one of the three main dishes. With a few exceptions, however, this book introduces only Japanese recipes.

Japanese cuisine is extremely healthful. The reasons being that Japanese use many foods such as tofu, seaweed and fish that are very nutritious but have a low caloric value. Foods are mainly grilled and boiled.

So if you are trying to control your weight, this is the book for you. Each recipe has the number of calories given for each single serving.

This book brings you recipes that can be prepared quickly using a regular or microwave oven; approximate preparation times for each recipe; and the most widely used seasonings on the market. Regarding costs, substitute ingredients have been given wherever possible as the prices of vegetables and fish fluctuate day by day. These costs are based on Tokyo prices. To help the reader when shopping, the names of foodstuffs are given in kanji and romaji. In all the recipes the quantities of ingredients are for four servings.

The authors, Miyoko Sakai and Motoko Abe, have lived overseas for varying periods. Sakai lived in the United States for two years and Thailand for three years, and Abe spent two years in Britain, the Philippines and Thailand respectively.

As a result of our experiences and acquaintance with foreign residents in Japan, we decided to put together a quick and easy Japanese cooking book in English. And here it is. Hopefully, it will help you add a little more variety to your dining table. Itadakimasu.

November 1989

Miyoko Sakai
Motoko Abe

Acknowledgments

We would like to thank all friends and the following companies for their cooperation.
Elizabeth Sharp
Satoru Oshima
Ryoko Yakata

Ajinomoto Co., Inc.
House Food Industrial Co., Ltd.
Kikkoman Corporation
MCC Food Products, Co., Ltd.
Nakano Vinegar Co., Ltd.
Nissin Food Products., Ltd.
Toshiba Corporation

Ingredients for Japanese Cooking

Japanese cooking seeks to preserve the natural taste of the ingredients, so it is extremely important to select fresh foods. The clue lies in choosing products that are in season. With the development of greenhouses and biotechnology, out of season vegetables are available all year around. When shopping, remember that the produce in season is the cheapest and also the most nutritious.

The most important flavorings in Japanese cuisine are soy sauce and *miso*, both of which are made from soybeans; and sake and *mirin* (sweet sake).

Soy sauce comes in two types: strong soy sauce, which is a blackish color and is used in everyday cooking, and weak soy sauce, which is lighter in color and saltier, and used mainly in the Kansai region. Weak soy sauce is suitable for clear soups and boiled vegetables. Kikkoman soy sauce is the best known brand abroad, but there are many other brands including Yamasa and Higeta.

Miso comes in three types: *Komemiso* is made from soybeans and white rice; examples are *Sendai-miso*, *Shinshū-miso*, and *Edo-miso*. *Shiromiso* is a type of *komemiso* that is widely used in the Kansai region; it is a whitish color because it uses about three times as much *koji* (malted rice). *Akamiso* is commonly used in the Kanto region; *mugimiso*, which is made from soybeans and barley, has a strong flavor; it is sometimes called *inakamiso*; and *mamemiso*, which is made only from soybeans. *Hatchōmiso* and *tamarimiso* are types of *mamemiso*.

Just as Westerners sometimes use wine to flavor their dishes, Japanese like to add a little sake to sweeten their cooking. *Mirin* is made by adding *kōji* and glutinous rice to *shōchū* (distilled liquor). Compared with sake, *mirin* is sweet and brings out the taste in the food.

One of the most popular spices used in Japan is *wasabi* (horseradish), a perennial plant of the crucifer family that grows by mountain streams. The grated root is used as a spice. About the size of a small carrot and colored green, the root adds fragrance and bitterness to food. Horseradish is especially used as an accompaniment to *sashimi* (raw fish) and *sushi*, because it removes the raw taste. It is available in powdered form or as a paste.

Sansho (Japanese pepper tree) is a deciduous tree belonging to the rue family; it has a distinctive smell and sharpness. The young leaf sprigs are used to garnish fried foods, and the pods are used as a spice.

Shichimi tōgarashi (seven-flavor spice) is a spice mixture composed of red pepper flakes together with *sansho* pods, sesame seeds, and other ingredients. The extremely sharp spice mixture is used with *soba* and *udon* noodles.

Shiso (perilla) has aromatic fruit and leaves that are used as a garnish with raw fish or as pickles. The leaves come in two colors, the green being used with raw food and the red to add color to plums, pickles and confectionery.

Yuzu (citron) and *sudachi* are members of the rue family. As with lemons, the peel and juice are used to add fragrance and bitterness to food.

Shōga (ginger) and *naganegi* (long onion) are finely

chopped and used in various sauces. They remove the strong smell of meat and fish. Like *shichimi tōgarashi*, these spices are called *yakumi*, which means that they are especially good for the health. (*Yaku* means medicine in Japanese.)

Marine plants are low in calories and hence good for the health. Some marine plants, such as *wakame* (seaweed), are eaten raw, vinegared, or in salads, while others are used as a garnish for raw fish. *Kombu* (kelp) is thick and hard; it is dried under the sun, and when used it is soaked in water, then boiled mainly for stock.

Nori is seaweed that has been drained, chopped into fine pieces, passed through a special combing machine, and dried. Lightly toasted, it is used to roll sushi or for *onigiri* (rice balls). Flavored *nori*, is dipped in soy sauce and eaten with rice.

Katsuobushi (dried bonito) is made by grilling bonito, drying it and then, shaving it into thin flakes using a special shredder. Dried bonito flakes come in packs.

Konnyaku is made from the root of the devil's tongue plant. Since it consists of 97% water and 2% sugar, it is an excellent diet food with no calories. *Konnyaku* that is made into fine threads is called *shirataki*.

Kampyō (gourd strips) is made by cutting the flesh of the gourd into long, thin pieces and drying them. *Kampyo* needs to be soaked in water before cooking it with seasonings. It is one of the ingredients for *sushi*.

Cooking utensils

Kitchen knife and cutting board
Japanese cooking places a lot of emphasis on the art of cutting. In the past, it was usual for households to have separate knives for cutting raw fish, slicing fish, and chopping vegetables. Most families today, however, make do with one knife with a round tip, called a *bunka hōchō*. When you cut food, you should use a cutting board, called a *manaita*. Both wooden and plastic cutting boards are available.

Grinder
A grinder (*suribachi and surikogi*) is used for crushing and grinding sesame seeds and other ingredients. Since most of these ground ingredients are available already ground, it is possible to manage without one.

Broiling net

A broiling net (*yakiami*) is used for broiling meat or fish. If you have a griller in your range you do not need a net. When using a broiling net, it is advisable to grease it so that the fish does not stick to it.

Grater

A grater (*oroshiki*) is necessary for grating horseradish, radish and ginger. Try and buy one with a saucer attached.

Microwave oven

Measurements

Weights and measures

1 cup = 200 ml
3 teaspoons (tsps) = 1 tablespoon (tbsp)
1 tbsp (tablespoon) = 15 ml
1 tsp (teaspoon) = 5 ml

Ingredient equivalents

radish	1 medium	800 g	40 cm
grated radish	1 cup	200 g	
burdock stick	1 medium	150 g	70 cm
carrot	1 medium	200 g	15 cm
long onion	1 medium	130 g	60 cm
snow peas	1 cup	80 g	
lotus root	1 cup chopped	140 g	
bamboo shoot	1 cup chopped	120 g	

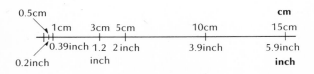

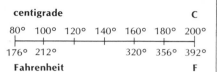

temperature

centigrade   **C**

80° 100° 120° 140° 160° 180° 200°

176° 212°   320° 356° 392°

Fahrenheit   **F**

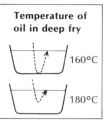

Temperature of
oil in deep fry

160°C

180°C

Put a pinch of batter into heated oil, if the oil is as high as 160°C, it will sink to the bottom of the pan and rise to the surface. If the oil is as high as 180°C, it will sink only half way before rising to the surface.

Explanation of ratings and symbols

All ratings and symbols are for one person.
Cooking time and cooking cost are each rated on a scale of A to D in columns marked **Time** and **Cost**.

Cooking time   A = less than 15 minutes
                   B = 15~30 minutes
                   C = 30 minutes~1 hour
                   D = more than 1 hour

Cooking cost   A = less than 100 yen
                   B = 100~200 yen
                   C = 200~300 yen
                   D = more than 300 yen

The cost reflects the estimated price at supermarkets in central Tokyo area.

The Calories column, headed **Cal.**, indicates figures for one person.

In all the recipes the quantities of ingredients are for four servings.

QUICK
&
EASY
JAPANESE
COOKING
FOR
EVERYONE

by Miyoko Sakai and Motoko Abe

The Japan Times

ISBN4-7890-0496-1

First edition: December 1989
7th printing: August 1994

Jacket design and Layout by CADEC, Inc.

Published by The Japan Times, Ltd.
5-4, Shibaura 4-chome, Minato-ku, Tokyo 108, Japan

Printed in Japan

1
Soup

There are two types of Japanese soup. One is a clear soup (*sumashi-jiru*), which looks like consommè. The other is soup made from soybean paste (*miso*) which resembles brown potage soup, and is called *misoshiru*.

In the making of soup stock (*dashi*) plays an important role. Japanese soup stock is made from dried kelp (*kombu*), dried bonito flakes (*katsuobushi*) or small dried fish (*niboshi*). Recently, most housewives tend to use instant stock and synthetic seasonings. In this book we prefer the easiest way, that is, using a granule-type seasoning (*dashinomoto*). This seasoning also comes in tea-bag and liquid forms.

Instant clear soup (*sumashi-jiru*) and *miso* soup (*miso-shiru*) are handy timesavers. Just add boiling water and mix well. If you want your speciality, add cooked meat, fish or vegetables.

Traditional method for making soup stock
(1)   For clear soup or *miso* soup
1)   Cut dried kelp (*kombu*) into 15-cm lengths. Tear in some places and wipe with a cloth or paper towel. Pour 4½ cups water into a pan and soak the kelp for 10 minutes.
2)   Heat water and kelp, just before it comes to the boil remove the kelp, then reduce heat, add 1 cup of dried bonito flakes (*katsuobushi*) and simmer for a minute, turn off heat and let it stand.
3)   When all bonito flakes have settled on the bottom of the pan, strain soup through a sieve with a

paper towel or cloth in it. This is the first soup stock (*ichiban dashi*).

4) Pour 2 cups of water into a pan and add the kelp and bonito flakes which have been used for the first soup stock. Bring the mixture to the boil and simmer for 5 minutes. Strain soup stock in the same way as Step 3 to make the second soup stock (*niban dashi*).

(2) For *miso* soup

1) Remove heads and guts from 20 small dried fish (*niboshi*), tear into halves. Pour 4½ cups water into a pan with the dried fish. (If you like a thick soup, 15 cm of kelp may be added, after wiping it with paper.) Bring water to the boil, remove kelp and simmer for 20 minutes.

2) Strain soup stock.

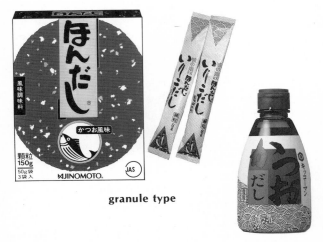

granule type

liquid form

1) Soak the kelp in water.

2) Remove kelp just before water boils.

2) Add dried bonito flakes.

2) Skim off scum.

3) Strain soup.

Remove heads and gut from *niboshi*

3

(1)—SOUP

1·Clear soup
[*Sumashi-jiru* すまし汁]

___

INGREDIENTS

4½ cups water
1 tsp *dashinomoto*
1 tsp salt
½ tsp soy sauce
80 g chicken (*tori sasami* トリささみ)
salt, sake and potato starch (*katakuriko* カタクリ粉) or cornstarch
4 Chinese black mushrooms (*shiitake* シイタケ)
8 snow peas (*sayaendō* サヤエンドウ)

1) Remove tendon from chicken and cut into 3-cm pieces. Season with a pinch of salt and sake and coat with potato starch.
2) Remove stems from mushrooms. Make a criss-cross incision on the top of mushrooms.
3) Trim snow peas.
4) Heat 2 cups of water in a saucepan. Boil chicken for 3 minutes, remove and drain. Add salt to water and blanch Chinese black mushrooms then string snow peas. Put chicken, mushrooms and snow peas into soup bowls.
5) Heat 4½ cups of water. Add *dashinomoto*, salt and soy sauce. Pour the piping hot soup into soup bowls.

NOTE

• Shrimps (*ebi*), tofu, long onion (*naganegi*), onion (*tamanegi*), trefoil (*mitsuba*), spinach (*hōrensō*), carrot (*ninjin*), radish (*daikon*), green peas (*guriin piisu*)

4

frozen or canned, fish cake (*kamaboko*), egg (*tamago*), boiled or scrambled can be substituted.

- **For microwave cooking:** Chicken, mushrooms and snow peas can be covered with plastic wrap and cooked for 3 minutes.

frozen snow peas

Cal.	Time	Cost
75	A	A

2·Miso soup
[*Miso-shiru* みそ汁]

INGREDIENTS

4½ cups water
1 tsp *dashinomoto*
4 tbsps *miso*
1 thin sheet deep fried tofu (*abura age* 油揚げ)
1 cup chopped radish (*daikon* ダイコン)
½ long onion (*naganegi* 長ネギ)

1) Cut thin deep fried tofu in half lengthwise then into 1-cm strips.
2) Peel radish, cut lengthwise and then cut into 1-cm strips. (see P. 128 E)
3) Cut long onion thinly crosswise.
4) Put 4½ cups of water with *dashinomoto*, deep fried tofu and radish into a saucepan. Boil until radish is done, skim off any scum that forms.
5) Place *miso* in a ladle, then put into the boiling soup and stir with chopsticks until dissolved. After soup comes to the boil, add long onion and turn off heat immediately.

NOTE

• Tofu, seaweed (*wakame*), Chinese cabbage (*hakusai*), onion (*tamanegi*), spinach (*hōrensō*), or Chinese black mushrooms (*shiitake*) can be substituted.

Cal.	Time	Cost
124	B	A

3·Pork *miso* soup
[*Ton-jiru* トン汁]

INGREDIENTS

100 g thinly sliced pork (*buta komagire* ブタこま切れ)
½ cup chopped radish (*daikon* ダイコン)
¼ carrot (*ninjin* ニンジン)
4 taros (*satoimo* サトイモ)
½ block *konnyaku* (コンニャク)
¼ cup chopped burdock stick (*gobō* ゴボウ)
2 tbsps chopped long onion (*naganegi* 長ネギ)
5 cups water
1 tsp *dashinomoto*
4 tbsps *miso*

1) Peel radish and carrot and cut into rounds then in-to quarters.
2) Peel burdock and cut crosswise into 3-cm lengths, then into 1-cm wide strips. Soak in water with 1 tsp vinegar for 10 minutes.
3) Peel taros and cut crosswise into half. Soak in water for 10 minutes.
4) Cut *konnyaku* into bite-size pieces. Boil for 3 minutes and drain.
5) Boil 5 cups of water. Add pork, burdock, carrot, radish, *konnyaku* and taros. Skim off any scum that forms. Boil until vegetables are cooked. Add long onion and 1 tsp *dashinomoto* and boil for 1 minute more.
6) Place *miso* in a ladle, then put into the boiling soup and stir with chopsticks until dissolved. When soup comes to the boil, turn off heat immediately.

2
Rice

In most Japanese homes rice is eaten every day. Plain white rice is one of the basic elements of the daily menu. There are two types of rice: one is a long grain, known as the Indica species and the other is short and thick, which is the Japonica species and is eaten in Japan.

In the past rice was cooked in a heavy iron pot (*kama*), but nowadays rice cookers are widely used. Rice cookers are convenient because they are automatic and keep the rice warm after it is cooked. You can choose the size of the cooker according to the number in the family.

(1) How to cook plain rice (for 4 people)
3 cups rice.
3¼ cups water
1) Wash rice thoroughly and drain. Place in rice cooker.
2) Pour 3¼ cups water over rice and soak for 30 minutes. If you don't like sticky rice, cook without soaking.
3) Cook in an electric rice cooker. If using a saucepan, cook rice over a high heat. When rice boils, turn heat to medium and cook for 2 minutes. Reduce heat to low and simmer for 15 minutes. Turn heat to high for 5 seconds, then turn off.
4) If any cooked rice is left, it is advisable to freeze it in portions of individual servings.

(2) How to cook *sushi* rice

3 cups rice

3 ¼ cups water

1) Follow Steps 1 and 2 for cooking rice.

2) Cut kelp (*kombu*) into 15-cm lengths and wipe with paper. Soak kelp in the washed rice for 30 minutes.

3) Remove kelp and pour 1 tbsp sake into the rice, then cook.

4) After rice is cooked, place in baking pan or shallow bowl and fan rice to cool it, then add seasoning. Measure 4½ tbsps rice vinegar, 1½ tsps salt and 2 tbsps sugar and mix well. Pour seasoning mixture over cooked rice. Mix well with a wet wooden spatula.

* You can buy instant packets of seasoning for *sushi* (*sushi no moto*). Add 3 tbsps of *sushi no moto* to rice and mix well.

sushi no moto

Cal.	Time	Cost
949	C	A

4·Vinegared rice wrapped in thin fried tofu
[*Inari-zushi* いなりずし]

INGREDIENTS

3 cups rice (*kome* 米)
12 sheets thin fried tofu (*abura age* 油揚げ)
1 cup water
½ cup sake
5 tbsps soy sauce
5 tbsps sugar
1 tbsp *mirin*

1) Cook 3 cups *sushi* rice (see P. 10).
2) Cut thin fried tofu in half and open the cut end to make a pocket. Boil water, add thin fried tofu and cook for 5 minutes and drain.
3) Bring 1 cup water to the boil, add sake, sugar, soy sauce and *mirin* then add the thin fried tofu. Simmer until all liquid has evaporated. Squeeze lightly to remove excess liquid.
4) Make 24 rice balls and put into the tofu bags.

NOTE

• Sliced lotus root (*renkon*), carrot (*ninjin*), or sesame seeds (*iri goma*) can be mixed into the *sushi* rice.
• Already prepared thin fried tofu for *inari-zushi* is available at supermarkets.

Cal.	Time	Cost
758	C	C

5·Hand wrapped sushi
[*Temaki-zushi* 手巻きずし]

INGREDIENTS

3 cups rice (*kome* 米)
200 g fresh tuna (*maguro no sashimi* マグロの刺し身)
8 shrimps (*ebi* エビ)
200 g squid (*sashimiyō ika* 刺し身用イカ)
50 g cod roe (*tarako* タラコ)
1 cucumber (*kyūri* キュウリ)
3 eggs (*tamago* 卵)
10 sheets dried seaweed (*yaki nori* 焼きノリ)
Japanese horseradish (*wasabi* ワサビ) powder or tube

1) Cook 3 cups *sushi* rice(see P. 10).
2) Cut tuna, squid and cucumber into 10-cm-long strips.
3) Insert toothpick under black vein of shrimps and remove the vein. Boil shrimps in water. Remove shells.
4) Cook rolled egg (see P. 67) and cut into 10-cm strips.
5) Cut seaweed into quarters.
6) Arrange ingredients on a plate.
7) Place *sushi* rice on seaweed and put one or more of the ingredients on the rice. For the seafood, spread a little Japanese horseradish on the rice. Wrap seaweed around rice and other ingredients and dip in soy sauce before eating.

- Smoked salmon (*sumōku sāmon*), cheese, canned salmon (*sake no kanzume*) — season with mayonnaise, crab (*kani*), avocado (*abokado*), perilla (*shiso*), or fermented soybeans (*nattō*) can be substituted.

* This type of *temaki-zushi* is for informal occasions.

Rolled *sushi* [*Norimaki*]

Place a sheet of seaweed (*nori*) on bamboo mat (*makisu*). With wet hands spread *sushi* rice over two-thirds of the seaweed leaving a little space at each end. Arrange, raw fish, egg and vegetables of *temaki-zushi* on rice. Lift bamboo mat with seaweed over ingredients and press, then roll.

Let roll stand for 5 minutes before cutting. When cutting *norimaki* wipe knife with wet cloth to stop rice from sticking to it.

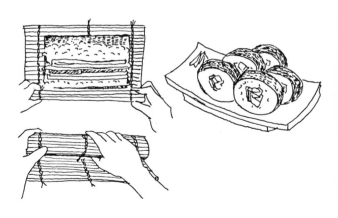

(2)— RICE

6·Sushi rice topped with vegetables and seafood
[*Chirashi-zushi* ちらしずし]

INGREDIENTS

3 cups rice (*kome* 米)
4 dried Chinese black mushrooms (*hoshi shiitake* 干しシイタケ)
½ carrot (*ninjin* ニンジン)
1 cup lotus root (*renkon* レンコン)
200 g shrimps (*ebi* エビ)
3 eggs (*tamago* 卵)
15 trefoil stalks (*mitsuba* ミツバ)

1) Soak Chinese black mushrooms in water until soft. Remove stems and boil mushrooms in the water they were soaked in with 1 tbsp sugar, 1 tbsp soy sauce and 2 tsps *mirin*. Cook until most of the liquid has evaporated. Cool, then cut lengthwise into 5-mm slivers.

2) Peel and cut carrot lengthwise then into 5-mm strips (see P. 128 E). Boil ⅔ cup water with 1 tsp sugar and a pinch of salt, add carrot and cook until liquid has nearly evaporated.

3) Peel lotus root and cut into 5-mm thick rings. Soak in water with 1 tsp vinegar for 5 minutes. Boil 1 cup water with 2 tbsps vinegar and ½ tsp salt and blanch lotus root. Drain and soak in sweetened vinegar (3 tbsps vinegar, 1½ tbsps sugar and ½ tsp salt) for 10 minutes.

4) Beat eggs lightly with a pinch of salt and 3 tsps sugar. Grease skillet and heat, excess oil should be

wiped off with kitchen paper, pour 3 tbsps egg mixture and spread over the bottom of the pan. Fry for 20 seconds and turn over. Repeat this process until all egg is used. Place thin sheets of fried egg on top of each other and slice into 5-mm strips.

5) Insert toothpick under black vein of shrimps and remove vein. Remove the shell leaving the tail intact. Boil 2 cups water, add shrimps, a pinch of salt and sake and boil for 3 minutes. Drain.

6) Cut trefoil into 10-cm lengths.

7) Cook *sushi* rice (see P. 10). Stir ⅔ of prepared ingredients into *sushi* rice. Garnish with leftover ingredients.

NOTE

- Crab meat (*kani*) or fish marinated in vinegar can be substituted.

(2)— RICE

7·Rice with mushrooms
[*Shimeji gohan* シメジごはん]

___

INGREDIENTS

3 cups rice (*kome* 米)
3 cups water
3 packs *shimeji* mushrooms (*shimeji* シメジ)
3 tbsps sake
1½ tbsps soy sauce
⅔ tsp salt

1) Wash rice. Soak in 3 cups water for 30 minutes in the rice cooker.
2) Remove stems from mushrooms. Sprinkle with 3 tbsps sake and 1½ tbsps soy sauce.
3) Put mushrooms with sake and soy sauce into rice and cook.
4) Cook rice in regular manner.

NOTE

- 2 sheets thin fried tofu (*abura age*). Blanch, cut in half and then into 5-mm slivers. Boil in ⅓ cup water with 2 tsps sugar, 2 tsps soy sauce and 1 tsp *mirin* and simmer until water has nearly evaporated. Mix into rice after it is cooked.
- Already prepared *takikomi gohan* is available at supermarkets.
- **Rice Cooked with Green Peas (*mame gohan*)**
  1½ cups frozen green peas (*guriin piisu*).
  Cook 3 cups rice and green peas with 3¼ cups water, 1 tsp *dashinomoto*, 2 tbsps sake and 2 tsps salt.

Cal.	Time	Cost
584	C	B

8·Rice with chicken and vegetables
[*Takikomi gohan* 炊き込みごはん]

INGREDIENTS

3 cups rice (*kome* 米)
1 tsp *dashinomoto*
1 tbsp soy sauce
150 g chicken breasts (*tori muneniku* トリ胸肉)
3 Chinese black mushrooms (*shiitake* シイタケ)
½ cup chopped burdock stick (*gobō* ゴボウ)
¼ carrot (*ninjin* ニンジン)
1 sheet thin fried tofu (*abura age* 油揚げ)

1) Wash rice and soak for 30 minutes before cooking.

2) Cut chicken into 1-cm cubes and soak in 2 tbsps soy sauce, 2 tbsps sake and 1 tbsp sugar. Let stand for 10 minutes and drain. Keep sauce for later use.

3) Remove stems from Chinese black mushrooms and cut into 5-mm strips. Soak thin fried tofu in boiling water for 30 seconds to remove some of the oil. Cut in half and then into 5-mm strips. Peel carrot and cut lengthwise and then into 5-mm strips (see P. 128 E). Remove skin from burdock and shave into thin slivers (see P. 128 F), soak in water with 1 tsp vinegar for 10 minutes.

4) Measure 3⅓ cups water, including the leftover soaking sauce, for boiling the rice. Add *dashinomoto* and soy sauce. Add chicken, vegetables and thin fried tofu to the rice and cook.

Cal.	Time	Cost
736	C	B

9·Beef bowl
[*Gyūdon* 牛丼]

> **INGREDIENTS**

3 cups rice (*kome* 米)
200 g sliced beef (*gyū usugiri niku* 牛薄切り肉)
1 onion (*tamanegi* タマネギ)
1 bunch spinach (*hōrensō* ホウレンソウ)
4 eggs (*tamago* 卵)
Sauce
    1 ½ cups water
    ½ tsp *dashinomoto*
    3 tbsps sugar
    5 tbsps *mirin*
    5 tbsps soy sauce

1) Cook rice.
2) Cut beef into 6-cm pieces.
3) Cut onion in half and slice.
4) Blanch spinach, drain, squeeze lightly and cut into 3-cm lengths.
5) Bring water with *dashinomoto* to the boil. Add sugar, *mirin* and soy sauce. Simmer until broth is reduced by half. Add beef and onions. Boil for 5 minutes and add spinach. Turn off heat.
6) Put a quarter of sauce with beef, onion and spinach into a small saucepan. Pour in 1 beaten egg, cover and simmer on moderate heat until the egg sets.
7) Put rice in large rice bowls (*donburi*) and top rice with beef and egg mixture.

- Use long onion instead of onion.
- *Shirataki* can be added.
- Ready-made *sukiyakidon no moto* or *gyudon no moto* are available at supermarkets.

5)-1   5)-2

6)   7)

Cal.	Time	Cost
697	C	B

10·Chicken and egg on rice
[*Oyako donburi* 親子丼]

INGREDIENTS

3 cups rice (*kome* 米)
200 g chicken breasts (*tori muneniku* トリ胸肉)
1 onion (*tamanegi* タマネギ)
4 eggs (*tamago* 卵)
12 trefoil stalks (*mitsuba* ミツバ)
½ cup frozen green peas (*guriin piisu* グリーンピース)
Sauce
    1½ cups water
    4 tbsps soy sauce
    4 tbsps sake
    3 tsps sugar

1) Cook rice.
2) Cut chicken into 2-cm cubes. Slice onions. Cut trefoil into 3-cm lengths.
3) Place sauce ingredients in pan with chicken, onion and green peas, cover with lid and cook until chicken is done. Turn off heat. Put a quarter of sauce with chicken and vegetables into a small pan. Pour in 1 beaten egg and simmer until egg is set, top with trefoil then turn off heat.
4) Put rice in large rice bowls (*donburi*) and top with chicken and egg mixture.

NOTE

•**Pork and egg on rice (*katsudon*)**
Cook pork cutlet (*tonkatsu*) (see P. 36) and 3 cups rice. Follow Steps 3 and 4 of above recipe.

20

•This recipe can be prepared omitting the chicken: *tamago donburi.*

Instant chicken and egg topping

11·Tricolor rice
[*Sanshoku gohan* 三色ごはん]

INGREDIENTS

3 cups rice (*kome* 米)
200 g minced beef (*gyū hikiniku* 牛ひき肉)
    2½ tbsps soy sauce
    3 tbsps *mirin*
    1 tbsp sugar
    2 tbsps sake
3 eggs (*tamago* 卵)
    salt and pepper
    2 tsps sugar
1 tbsp vegetable oil
1 cup string beans (*sayaingen* サヤインゲン)

1) Cook plain white rice.
2) Sauté beef with soy sauce, *mirin*, sugar and sake over a medium heat until water has evaporated.
3) In a bowl, beat lightly together eggs, salt, pepper and sugar. Heat oil in a skillet and pour in egg mixture, using chopsticks scramble egg over medium heat until cooked.
4) Cut string beans on the slant and boil in salted water until soft. Drain.
5) Put rice in large rice bowls (*donburi*) and top with minced beef, egg and string beans.

NOTE

• Rice can be cooked with 2 tbsps soy sauce, 1½ tbsps sake and a pinch of salt.

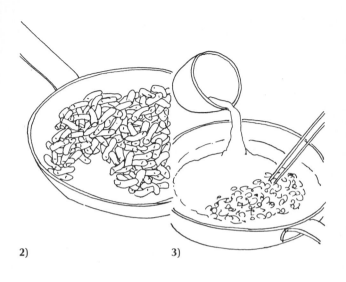

2)

3)

4)

(2)—RICE

12·Fried rice
[*Chāhan* チャーハン]

INGREDIENTS

3 cups rice (*kome* 米) or 4 bowls cooked rice
60 g ham (*hamu* ハム)
¼ can crab meat (*kani no kanzume* カニの缶詰)
⅓ long onion (*naganegi* 長ネギ)
2 eggs (*tamago* 卵)
4 tbsps vegetable oil
2 tbsps sesame oil
1 tbsp soy sauce

1) Cook rice, or use leftover cooked rice.
2) Chop ham and long onion. Remove cartilage from crab meat.
3) Put 2 tbsps vegetable oil in a pan and heat. Pour in lightly beaten eggs and fry. When egg is done, push it to the edge of the pan. Add 2 more tbsps vegetable oil and add cooked rice, season with salt and pepper. Turn heat to high and fry rice and egg. When rice is dry, add ham, crab meat and long onion. Add soy sauce and 2 tbsps sesame oil. Stir well.

NOTE

• 3 Chinese black mushrooms chopped (*shiitake*), ¼ carrot chopped (*ninjin*), 3 green peppers chopped (*piiman*), 15 snow peas chopped (*sayaendō*), frozen mixed vegetables or any leftover meat and vegetables can be used.

Cal.	Time	Cost
200	A	A

13·Rice gruel
[*Zōsui* 雑炊]

INGREDIENTS

2 bowls cooked rice (*gohan* ごはん)
200 g chicken breasts (*tori muneniku* トリ胸肉)
⅓ small radish (*daikon* ダイコン)
1 bunch trefoil stalks (*mitsuba* ミツバ)
6 cups water
1½ tsps *dashinomoto*
salt
2 tbsps soy sauce

1) Place cooked rice in a sieve and wash under running water to make rice less sticky.
2) Cut chicken into 3-cm cubes. Cut radish into 5-cm strips. Cut trefoil into 10-cm lengths.
3) Boil water and *dashinomoto*. Add washed rice chicken and radish, and simmer for 5 minutes. Season with salt and soy sauce. Decorate with trefoil before serving.

NOTE

• Shrimps (*ebi*), crab (*kani*), or any fish can be substituted.
• Long onion (*naganegi*), or chrysanthemum leaves (*shungiku*) are also suitable.
• Egg can be added.
• Leftover rice, meat and vegetables can also be used.
• This rice gruel is good for breakfast, midnight snacks and baby food.

3
Meat

In Japan the butcher trims and slices the meat ready for sale, but if the right cut can't be found, ask the butcher to prepare the meat to your requirements. Generally speaking, beef (*gyūniku*) is very expensive, especially the beef raised here which is called *wagyū*. Wagyū is used in dishes like *sukiyaki* and *shabushabu* because it is extremely tender. Pork (*butaniku*) is more economical than beef and is used in many Japanese recipes. Chicken (*toriniku*) is the most affordable of all the meats and you get an added bonus as it is high in protein and low in calories. Chicken, like other meats, is already prepared in cuts. If a whole chicken is required it is wise to order it in advance.

In earlier times Japanese didn't consume very much meat and dishes consisted mainly of chicken and wild duck. Nowadays, meat is quite popular and Japanese have adapted dishes from the West and China to suit their tastes by using seasonings such as soy sauce, *mirin*, *miso* and sake.

(3)—MEAT

14·Grilled chicken on skewers
[*Yakitori* 焼きトリ]

INGREDIENTS

400 g chicken thighs (*tori momoniku* トリもも肉)
2 long onion sticks (*naganegi* 長ネギ)
Yakitori sauce (*tare* たれ)
    4 tbsps soy sauce
    4 tbsps *mirin*
    2 tbsps sugar
8 bamboo skewers (*take gushi* 竹串) 12-cm long

1) Put ingredients for *yakitori* sauce into a saucepan and simmer until the amount is reduced by half.
2) Soak bamboo skewers in salted water to prevent them from burning.
3) Cut chicken into 3-cm cubes. Cut long onion into 3-cm lengths. Thread three pieces of chicken and 3 pieces of onion alternately onto skewers.
4) Preheat oven to 200° C. Arrange skewers in a single layer in greased baking pan and cook for 5 minutes. Dip chicken and long onion into *yakitori* sauce, return to pan and cook until done. Before serving, pour the leftover sauce over chicken.

NOTE

• Green pepper (*piiman*) or Chinese black mushrooms (*shiitake*) can be used instead.

3)

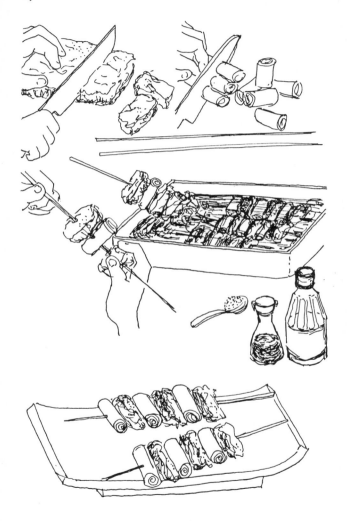

(3)—MEAT

15·Steamed chicken with sake
[*Tori no saka mushi* トリの酒蒸し]

INGREDIENTS

400 g chicken breasts (*tori muneniku* トリ胸肉)
2 tbsps sake
1 tbsp lemon juice
salt
Sauce

    2 tbsps sake
    2 tbsps soy sauce
    1 tbsp rice vinegar
    1 tsp sesame oil

1) Prick chicken breasts with a fork. Season with salt.
2) Put chicken in a small bowl and add sake and lemon juice, let chicken marinate for 20 minutes.
3) Place chicken and marinade in a steamer (*mushiki*) and steam for 20 minutes.
4) Mix together ingredients for the sauce and boil until sauce thickens.
5) Cut chicken into 1-cm pieces and serve with the sauce.

NOTE

- **For oven cooking:** Preheat oven to 200° C. Place bowl with chicken in it in a baking pan half filled with boiling water and cook for 20 minutes.
- **For microwave cooking:** Cover chicken and marinade and cook for 7 minutes.

(3)—MEAT

16·Chicken balls
[*Tori no tsukune* トリのつくね]

INGREDIENTS

300 g minced chicken (*tori hikiniku* トリひき肉)
1 small onion (*tamanegi* タマネギ)
½ tsp salt
3 tbsps sake
vegetable oil
Sauce
    ½ cup water
    1 tbsp sake
    2 tbsps sugar
    2 tbsps soy sauce
    1 tsp potato starch (*katakuriko* カタクリ粉)

1) Chop onion. Mix minced chicken, chopped onion, salt and sake and shape into 3-cm-diameter balls. Coat with potato starch.
2) Heat vegetable oil in a frying pan and deep fry chicken balls until light brown.
3) In a saucepan mix all ingredients for the sauce excluding the potato starch, add chicken balls and simmer for 5 minutes. Dissolve potato starch in 1 tbsp water, add to sauce and simmer until sauce thickens.

NOTE

• Chicken balls can be boiled with sauce made of ½ cup water, ¼ cup ketchup, 2 tbsps Worcestershire sauce, and 1 tbsp sake or ready-made barbecue sauce.

(3)—MEAT

17·Grilled chicken
[*Tori no momo yaki* トリのもも焼き]

INGREDIENTS

4 chicken thighs on the bone (*tori honetsuki momoniku* トリ骨付きもも肉)
Marinade
 ⅓ cup soy sauce
 2 tbsps *mirin*
 1 tbsp sugar
1 tbsp freshly grated ginger (*oroshi shōga* おろしショウガ)

1) Prick chicken with a fork to allow seasonings to be absorbed.
2) Peel and grate ginger. Marinate chicken in the sauce with the ginger for 1 hour turning occasionally. Drain.
3) Preheat oven to 200° C. Grill chicken in a baking pan for 20 minutes basting occasionally with the sauce.

NOTE

- Ready-made *teriyaki* sauce may be used.
- Boneless chicken is also suitable.
- **For microwave cooking:** Place chicken on a paper towel and place in a bowl, sprinkle with 1 tbsp of the leftover sauce and 1 tbsp vegetable oil and cook uncovered in microwave oven for 10 minutes.

18·Fried chicken with ginger
[*Tori no kara age* トリのから揚げ]

INGREDIENTS

600 g chicken thighs (*tori momoniku* トリもも肉)
Sauce
    2 tbsps sake
    2 tbsps soy sauce
    ginger juice (*shōga jiru*　ショウガ汁)
potato starch (*katakuriko*　カタクリ粉　) or cornstarch
vegetable oil

1) Peel and grate ginger then squeeze to extract the juice, mix with ingredients for sauce.
2) Cut chicken into 3-cm cubes and soak in sauce for 30 minutes, turning occasionally.
3) Sprinkle potato starch over chicken and mix by hand.
4) Heat vegetable oil to 180° C in a frying pan and deep fry, four chicken pieces at a time until golden brown. Repeat until all the chicken is cooked.

NOTE

- Use ready-made *kara ageko* instead of sauce and potato starch.
- Garlic can be used instead of ginger juice.

Cal.	Time	Cost
240	C	B

19 · Braised chicken and vegetables
[*Iridori* 炒りドリ]

INGREDIENTS

200 g chicken thighs (*tori momoniku* トリもも肉)
½ burdock stick (*gobō* ゴボウ)
1 cup lotus root (*renkon* レンコン)
1 carrot (*ninjin* ニンジン)
½ block *konnyaku* (コンニャク)
4 Chinese black mushrooms (*shiitake* シイタケ)
16 snow peas (*sayaendō* サヤエンドウ)
Sauce for chicken
    2 tbsps sake
    2 tbsps sugar
    2 tbsps soy sauce
Sauce
    2 cups water
    2 tbsps sugar
    2 tbsps *mirin*
    3 tbsps soy sauce
3 tbsps vegetable oil

1) Peel burdock and lotus root and cut into bite-size pieces and soak in water with 1 tsp vinegar for 5 minutes. Peel carrot and cut into bite-size pieces. Cut Chinese black mushrooms into quarters.

2) Cut *konnyaku* into bite-size pieces. Blanch in boiling water and drain. Remove strings from snow peas and blanch in boiling salted water.

3) Cut chicken into cubes. Sprinkle with sake and soy sauce. Bring 2 tbsps sake, 2 tbsps sugar and 2 tbsps

soy sauce to the boil then add chicken, simmer for 3 minutes.

4) Heat 3 tbsps vegetable oil in a saucepan. Sauté burdock, lotus root, carrot, *konnyaku* and Chinese black mushrooms for 3 minutes. Add 2 cups water and chicken with sauce to vegetables. Add sugar, *mirin* and soy sauce. Put aluminum foil over chicken and water then cover with a lid. Simmer for 20 minutes until broth has nearly evaporated.

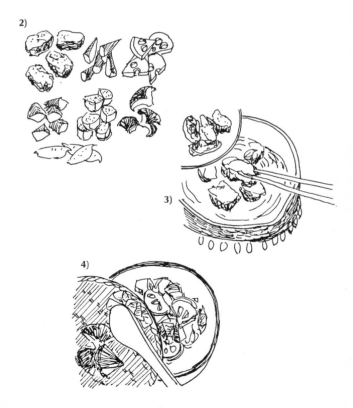

2)

3)

4)

Cal.	Time	Cost
587	B	C

20·Pork cutlets
[*Tonkatsu* トンカツ]

INGREDIENTS

4 pork loin cutlets (*buta tonkatsu yō kirimi* ブタトンカツ
用切り身)
1-cm thick, 120 g each
salt and pepper, garlic (optional)
flour (*komugiko* コムギ粉)
breadcrumbs (*panko* パン粉)
1 egg (*tamago* 卵)
vegetable oil
4 cabbage leaves (*kyabetsu* キャベツ)
ready-made sauce for *tonkatsu* (*tonkatsu sōsu* トンカツ
ソース)
mustard (*karashi* カラシ)

1) Make incision on fat and fiber. Sprinkle with salt
   and pepper. Rub in garlic (optional).
2) Coat pork with flour. Dip pork into mixture of
   beaten egg and 1 tsp water. Coat with breadcrumbs.
3) In a deep pan heat vegetable oil to 180° C. Deep
   fry pork until golden brown on both sides.
4) Serve pork with shredded cabbage. Eat pork with
   tonkatsu sauce and mustard.

NOTE

- Chicken can be substituted for pork. Ready-made
  tonkatsu sauce is recommended.
- Fish, such as salmon (*sake*), cod (*tara*), horse
  mackerel (*aji*) and squid (*ika*) are also suitable.

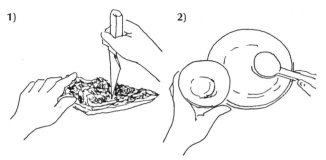

Pound with meat mallet.

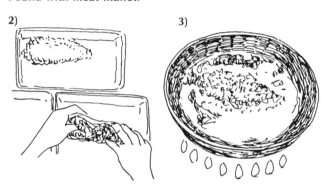

Beat egg and water together.

Deep fry.

Serve with shredded cabbage.

Ready-made *tonkatsu* sauce

(3)— MEAT

21·Boiled pork
[*Yudebuta* ゆでブタ]

INGREDIENTS

400 g pork loin in piece (*buta rōsu katamari* ブタロース
かたまり)
2 cloves garlic (*nin-niku* ニンニク)
2-cm piece fresh ginger (*shōga* ショウガ)
1 long onion (*naganegi* 長ネギ)
salt
4 tbsps sake
Garnish
    ½ radish (*daikon* ダイコン)
    1 cucumber (*kyūri* キュウリ)
    2 tomatoes (*tomato* トマト)
    10 lettuce leaves (*retasu* レタス)
Miso and vinegar-flavored sauce
    4 tbsps *miso*
    1 tbsp sugar
    2 tbsps sake
    2 tbsps vinegar
    2 tbsps water
    1 tsp mustard
Mayonnaise flavored sauce
    6 tbsps mayonnaise
    1 tbsp pickles (chopped)
    1 tsp onion (chopped)
Soy sauce with vinegar flavor
    2 tbsps chopped long onion (*naganegi* 長ネギ)
    1 tbsp chopped ginger (*shōga* ショウガ)
    2 tbsps soy sauce
    2 tbsps vinegar
    1 tsp sugar   2 tbsps sake

1) Rub garlic into pork. Sprinkle with salt. Tie pork with string. Slice ginger and cut long onion into 3-cm lengths.
2) Put pork in a strainer and pour boiling water over it for 30 seconds.
3) Pour enough water into the saucepan to cover the pork, add ginger, long onion, and 4 tbsps sake. After it boils, skim off any scum that forms, turn heat to low and cover pan. Simmer for 1 hour.
4) Cut radish lengthwise then cut into thin strips. Slice cucumber. Cut tomatoes and lettuce into segments.
5) Mix together ingredients for sauce.
6) Slice boiled pork into 5-mm rounds.
7) Serve on bed of lettuce and garnish with radish, cucumber and tomatoes.

Tea-flavored pork
[*Buta no kōcha ni*]

1) Tie 400g pork piece with string. Blanch pork and drain.

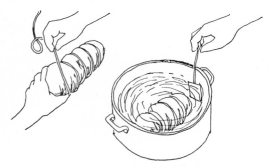

2) Cover pork with water, boil with tea bag for 1 hour.

3) Soak pork overnight in sauce in a ratio of soy sauce (4) to *mirin* (2) to rice vinegar (1).
   Quantity of liquid should be enough to cover pork.

4) **Remove string from pork and slice.**
   Place on a platter, garnish with *kaiware*, sliced long
   onion and black roasted sesame seeds.
   Pour the leftover soaking sauce.

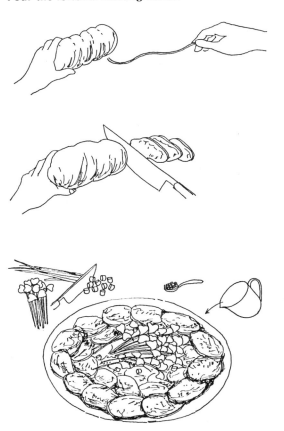

(3)—MEAT

22·Broiled pork Chinese style [*Yakibuta* 焼きブタ]

INGREDIENTS

400 g pork in piece (*buta momoniku katamari* ブタもも
肉かたまり)
salt and pepper
Sauce
    1 cup soy sauce
    1½ cups sake
    1 tbsp sugar
3 tbsps vegetable oil

1) Rub salt and pepper into pork. Tie pork with string.
2) Heat vegetable oil in a small saucepan, add pork and sauté until light brown.
3) Add ingredients for sauce, simmer on medium heat with lid on until liquid has almost evaporated, turning pork occasionally.
4) Remove string from pork and slice thinly before serving.
* *Yakibuta* can be used in Chinese noodles, fried rice and sandwiches.

Cal.	Time	Cost
341	B	B

23 · Broiled pork with *miso*
[*Butaniku no miso yaki* ブタ肉のみそ 焼き]

INGREDIENTS

400 g sliced pork (*buta usugiri niku* ブタ薄切り肉)
2 onions (*tamanegi* タマネギ)
2 green peppers (*piiman* ピーマン)
Marinade
    5 tbsps *miso*
    3 tbsps sake
    1 tbsp soy sauce
    1 tbsp sugar
    1 tsp freshly grated ginger (*oroshi shōga* おろしシ ョウガ)
vegetable oil

1) Mix together ingredients for marinade and marinate pork for 30 minutes.
2) Slice onions 5-mm thick and separate into rings. Slice green peppers in the same way as the onion.
3) Place greased aluminum foil in a baking pan and add pork, marinade and the vegetables.
4) Preheat oven to 200° C and cook pork and vegetables for 20 minutes.
5) Serve pork and vegetables with the sauce they were cooked in.

Cal.	Time	Cost
301	B	B

24 · Pork with ginger
[*Butaniku no shōga yaki*　ブタ肉のショウガ焼き]

INGREDIENTS

400 g sliced pork (*buta usugiri niku*　ブタ薄切り肉)
2 tbsps vegetable oil
Sauce
　　4 tbsps soy sauce
　　2 tbsps sake
1 tsp freshly grated ginger (*oroshi shōga*　おろしショウガ)

1) Mix together ingredients for sauce and grated ginger and marinate pork for 30 minutes turning occasionally. Drain.
2) Heat vegetable oil in a frying pan and sauté pork.

NOTE

- Cabbage (*kyabetsu*), bean sprouts (*moyashi*), onion (*tamanegi*) and green pepper (*piiman*) can be sautéd with the pork.

grating ginger

Cal.	Time	Cost
545	D	B

25 · Meat croquettes
[*Korokke* コロッケ]

INGREDIENTS

2 medium-size potatoes (*jagaimo* ジャガイモ)
300 g minced pork, minced beef or minced beef and pork (*buta hikiniku* ブタひき肉 , *gyū hikiniku* 牛ひき肉 , *aibiki* あいびき)
1 small onion (*tamanegi* タマネギ)
flour
salt and pepper
1 egg
breadcrumbs (*panko* パン粉)
vegetable oil

1) Peel potatoes and cut into segments. Boil and mash potatoes.
2) Chop onion.
3) Heat 1 tbsp vegetable oil in a saucepan, sauté chopped onion for 5 minutes, add minced meat. Sauté meat until light brown. Season meat mixture with salt and pepper and add 1 tbsp flour. Add mashed potato, egg yolk, stir and cook for 30 seconds. Mix well.
4) Divide potato and meat mixture into 8 portions and shape into 8 croquettes.
5) Dredge with flour. Dip into mixture of 1 egg white and 1 tbsp water. Coat with breadcrumbs.
6) In a deep pan heat 3 cups oil to 180° C (see P. xvii). Deep fry until golden brown.
7) Drain on kitchen paper.

Cal.	Time	Cost
808	C	B

(3)—MEAT

26·Pork curry
[*Karē raisu* カレーライス]

INGREDIENTS

300 g cubed pork (*buta* karēyō　ブタカレー用)
1 onion (*tamanegi* タマネギ)
2 potatoes (*jagaimo* ジャガイモ)
1 carrot (*ninjin* ニンジン)
2 tbsps vegetable oil
1 packet curry roux
3 cups rice
Condiments
　　pickles (*fukujinzuke*)
　　pickled scallion (*rakkyō*)
　　red pickled ginger (*beni shōga*)

1) Cook 3 cups rice.
2) Season pork with salt and pepper and coat with flour.
3) Cut onion into halves and slice thickly.
4) Peel potatoes and cut into bite-size pieces. Soak in water for 5 minutes.
5) Peel carrot and cut into rounds.
6) Heat vegetable oil in a saucepan. Sauté pork until brown. Add vegetables and sauté.
7) Add 3 cups water to the saucepan and boil. Skim off any scum that forms. Simmer for 20 minutes. Lower heat and add curry roux, stir until mixture thickens. Simmer for another 10 minutes.
8) Place rice in a soup bowl and top with pork curry.

- Curry roux comes in three types, mild (*amakuchi*), hot (*chūkara*) and very hot (*karakuchi*).

curry roux (mild, hot, very hot)

1) **Put pork and flour into plastic bag to shake.**

2) **Sauté pork then vegetables.**   3) **Add curry roux.**

47

Cal.	Time	Cost
444	C	B

27 · Beef and potato stew
[*Nikujaga* 肉ジャガ]

INGREDIENTS

300 g sliced beef (*gyū usugiri niku* 牛薄切り肉)
3 medium-size potatoes (*jagaimo* ジャガイモ)
1 onion (*tamanegi* タマネギ)
1 tbsp vegetable oil
2 cups water
3 tbsps sake
5 tbsps sugar
1 tbsp *mirin*
5 tbsps soy sauce

1) Peel potatoes and cut into six and soak in water for 5 minutes. Cut onion in half and slice. Cut beef into 7-cm pieces.

2) Heat 1 tbsp oil in a saucepan. Sauté beef until light brown, add potatoes and onion. Continue to sauté for 2 minutes.

3) Add 2 cups water and boil, skim off any scum that forms. Add sake, sugar, *mirin* and 2 tbsps soy sauce. Turn heat to low and cover ingredients in saucepan with aluminum foil and a lid. When potatoes are done, pour in remaining soy sauce and cook for 1 more minute.

NOTE

• Sliced pork (*buta usugiri niku*) can be a tasty change from beef.

Cal.	Time	Cost
187	A	D

28 · Rare beef
[*Gyūniku no tataki*　牛肉のたたき]

INGREDIENTS

500 g beef in piece (*gyū momoniku katamari*　牛もも肉かたまり)
salt and pepper
2 chives (*asatsuki*　アサツキ)
1 clove garlic
1 tsp freshly grated ginger (*oroshi shōga* おろしショウガ)
3 tbsps sake
3 tbsps soy sauce

1) Rub salt and pepper into beef just before cooking. Crush garlic and finely chop chives.
2) Heat 2 tbsps oil in a saucepan. Sauté beef on high heat until light brown. Add sake and soy sauce. Cover with a lid and steam for about 8 minutes on a low heat. Remove beef from pan. Boil broth for 2 minutes, pour over beef. When beef cools, slice as thinly as possible.
3) Garnish with chives, garlic and ginger.

NOTE

- Perilla (*shiso*) and parsely (*paseri*) can also be added.
- A salad can be made with ready-made rare beef (available at the supermarket) and vegetables such as cucumber (*kyūri*) and radish sprouts (*kaiware*).

29·Rolled beef
[*Yahata maki* 八幡巻き]

INGREDIENTS

300 g sliced beef (*gyū usugiri niku* 牛薄切り肉)
⅓ burdock stick (*gobō* ゴボウ)
½ carrot (*ninjin* ニンジン)
1 cup string beans (*sayaingen* サヤインゲン)
1 cup water
2 tbsps soy sauce
1 tbsp *mirin*
1 tsp sake
2 tbsps vegetable oil
Sauce
    3 tbsps soy sauce
    1 tbsp *mirin*
    1 tbsp sugar
    1 tbsp sake

1) Remove skin from burdock and cut into thin strips. Soak in water with 1 tsp vinegar for 10 minutes. Drain.

2) Boil 1 cup water with soy sauce, *mirin* and sake, add burdock and carrot. Simmer for 10 minutes.

3) Remove ends and strings from beans and boil in salted water for 3 minutes then drain.

4) Spread out beef and place burdock, carrot and beans at the edge then roll beef and secure with a toothpick.

5) Heat oil in a saucepan. Sauté rolled beef until all sides are light brown.

6) Mix ingredients for sauce and pour over rolled beef, cook until liquid has evaporated and meat is

cooked.

7) Take out toothpicks and cut rolls in half.

• Sliced pork (*buta usugiri niku*) can replace beef.

4)

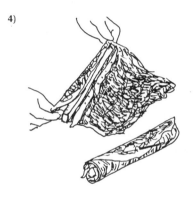

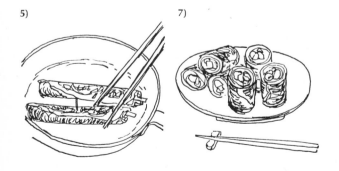

(3)—MEAT

30·Steak Japanese style
[*Wafū sutēki* 和風ステーキ]

INGREDIENTS

4 steaks (*gyū sutēki yō* 牛ステーキ用)
salt and pepper
2 tbsps oil
3 tbsps sake
3 tbsps soy sauce
½ lemon
½ cup grated radish (*daikon oroshi* ダイコンおろし)

1) Sprinkle salt and pepper over beef. Peel radish and grate finely.
2) Put 2 tbsps oil in a pan and heat. Sauté beef on a high heat until light brown, turn and sauté other side. Reduce heat, pour sake over steak and set aflame. Add soy sauce, simmer until sauce has evaporated.
3) Garnish with grated radish and sliced lemon.

NOTE
• Ready-made *teriyaki* sauce can be substituted for sake and soy sauce.

4
Seafood

Japanese eat many types of seafood, which is considered a staple of their diet. The way seafood is prepared is often determined by the seasons and the individual family's tastes.

Sashimi is one of the most popular seafood dishes in Japan and is eaten raw after being dipped in a mixture of soy sauce and Japanese horseradish (*wasabi*). The most popular types of fish used for *sashimi* are tuna (*maguro*), bonito (*katsuo*), baby yellowtail (*hamachi*), sea bream (*tai*), squid (*ika*) and boiled octopus (*tako*). Already prepared *sashimi* is available at supermarkets. Fishmongers will also prepare this dish on an order basis.

Radish (*daikon*), seaweed or perilla (*shiso*) are tasty garnishes for *sashimi* and other seafood dishes. These garnishes aid digestion.

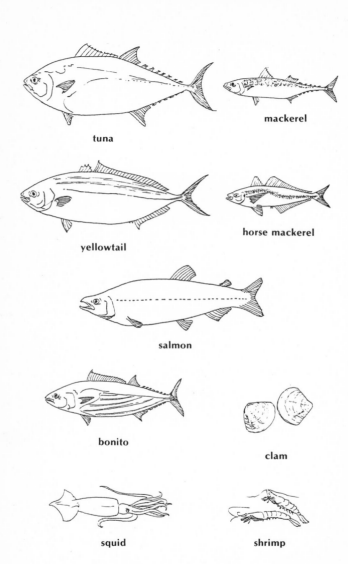

tuna

mackerel

yellowtail

horse mackerel

salmon

bonito

clam

squid

shrimp

Cal.	Time	Cost
102	B	C

31·Broiled salted fish
[*Sakana no shio yaki* 魚の塩焼き]

INGREDIENTS

4 horse mackerel (*aji* アジ)
salt
½ cup grated radish (*daikon oroshi* ダイコンおろし)
½ lemon

1) When purchasing whole fish, ask the fishmonger to prepare it for broiling. Sprinkle salt over fish. Sprinkle salt thickly over fins and tail, or cover with aluminum foil so they don't burn during cooking. Let fish stand for 20 minutes.

2) Place fish on a broiling net (*sakana yaki ami*) and broil on a high heat until dark brown. Turn and cook other side.

3) Peel radish and grate finely. Cut lemon into four segments.

4) Serve fish with grated radish and lemon. Pour soy sauce over fish, before eating.

NOTE

• Pacific saury (*sanma*), which is an autumn fish, sea bream (*tai*), cod (*tara*), mackerel (*saba*) are recommended.

• Fillet fish such as cod (*tara*), salmon (*sake*), Spanish mackerel (*sawara*), yellowtail (*buri*) can also be used.

• **For oven cooking:** Preheat oven to 200° C. Place fish on greased aluminum foil and cook for 15 minutes, turn and cook for another 5 minutes.

Cal.	Time	Cost
181	B	C

32·Teriyaki fish
[*Sakana no teriyaki* 魚の照り焼き]

INGREDIENTS

4 fillets Spanish mackerel (*sawara* サワラ)
Marinade
    2 tbsps *mirin*
    3 tbsps soy sauce
flour
3 tbsps vegetable oil
Sauce
    2 tbsps sugar
    1 tbsp *mirin*
    1 tbsp soy sauce

Marinate fish

1) Marinate fish in *mirin* and soy sauce for 30 minutes.

2) Wipe fish with paper towel and dust with flour. Put 3 tbsps vegetable oil into pan. Sauté fish until golden brown, shaking the pan to prevent fish from sticking. Turn over and reduce heat a little. Sauté until done. Mix together ingredients for sauce.

3) Pour the leftover marinade and sauce over the fish and boil until sauce thickens, shaking the pan occasionally.

NOTE

• For a sauce variation mix together 3 tbsps ketchup, 2 tbsps sake, 1 tbsp *mirin* and 1 tbsp soy sauce.

Cal.	Time	Cost
222	B	C

33·Broiled fish with lemon
[*Sakana no yūan-yaki* 魚のゆうあん 焼き]

INGREDIENTS

4 yellowtail fillets (*buri* ブリ)
Marinade
    2 tbsps sake
    2 tbsps *mirin*
    3 tbsps soy sauce
1 citron (*yuzu* ユズ) or ⅔ lemon (*remon* レモン)

1) Mix together marinade ingredients.
2) Add fish to marinade. Put sliced citron on top of yellowtail and marinate for several hours, turning occasionally.
3) Drain yellowtail and using a broiling net, broil the fish until golden brown. Turn and cook other side.

NOTE

- Spanish mackerel (*sawara*), salmon (*sake*), pomfret (*managatsuo*) are also suitable.
- **For oven cooking:** Preheat oven to 200° C and place fish on greased aluminum foil in a baking pan and cook for 20 minutes.

Cal.	Time	Cost
239	C	C

34 · Marinated fish
[*Ko aji no nanban zuke* 小アジの 南蛮漬け]

INGREDIENTS

8 small horse mackerel (*ko aji* 小アジ)
vegetable oil
potato starch (*katakuriko* カタクリ粉) or cornstarch
1 long onion (*naganegi* 長ネギ)
Marinade
6 tbsps soy sauce
6 tbsps rice vinegar
1 tbsp sugar
2 dried chili peppers (*aka tōgarashi* 赤トウガラシ)

1) Cut long onion into 3-cm lengths. Broil over an open flame until brown, turning occasionally.
2) Remove seeds from dried chili peppers and slice thinly. Boil marinade ingredients except chili peppers for 1 minute then stir in chili peppers and long onion.
3) Ask the fishmonger to prepare the horse mackerel for frying. Dust fish with potato starch. Deep fry over a low heat for 6 minutes. Turn heat to high and fry for another 30 seconds to make fish crisp. Turn off heat.
4) Put fish into marinade and leave for several hours.

NOTE

• Smelt (*wakasagi*) or sardines (*iwashi*) are also suitable.

58

Cal.	Time	Cost
53	B	B

35·Broiled squid
[*Ika no matsukasa yaki* イカの松かさ 焼き]

INGREDIENTS

300 g squid* (*ika* イカ)
4 tbsps soy sauce
2 tbsps *mirin*

1) Rub squid with cloth or paper towel to remove thin outer skin. Cut squid along gristle and open up, then make lengthwise and crosswise slashes on the squid.
2) Stick bamboo skewers into it to prevent squid from curling up when cooking.
3) Mix together soy sauce and *mirin*.
4) Broil squid on a broiling net (*sakana yaki ami*) until light brown. Turn and cook other side while basting occasionally with soy sauce mixture.
5) Cut into 8-cm squares.
* *Mongō ika* (cuttlefish) or *yari ika* (soft meat squid) is recommended.

NOTE

• **For oven cooking:** Preheat oven to 220° C, cook squid for 10 minutes, while basting with soy souce mixture.

1)

(4)—SEAFOOD

36·Broiled clams
[*Hamaguri no saka mushi* ハマグリ の酒蒸し]

INGREDIENTS

12 medium-size clams (*hamaguri* ハマグリ)
4 tbsps sake
soy sauce

1) Soak clams overnight in 3 cups water with 1 tbsp salt to remove sand.
2) Clean shells and cut off hinge with a knife. Place clams in a bowl and add 4 tbsps sake.
3) Steam clams in steamer for 7 minutes. Serve with soy sauce.

NOTE

• **For microwave cooking:** Place clams in bowls and add 4 tbsps sake. Cover and cook for 2 minutes.

37 · *Tempura*
[テンプラ]

> INGREDIENTS

8 large shrimps (*ebi* エビ)
4 small horse mackerel (*ko aji* ン)
4 Chinese black mushrooms (*shiita* ──ケ)
2 eggplants (*nasu* ナス)
½ sweet potato (*satsumaimo* サツマイモ)
2 small green peppers (*piiman* ピーマン)
Batter (*koromo* コロモ)
   1 cup flour
   1 egg and enough iced water to make 1 cup
Dipping sauce for *tempura* (*tentsuyu* 天つゆ)
   1 cup water
   ½ tsp *dashinomoto*
   ¼ cup soy sauce
   ¼ cup *mirin*
Condiments
   ½ cup grated radish (*daikon oroshi* ダイコンおろし)
   1 tbsp freshly grated ginger (*oroshi shōga* おろしショウガ)
3 cups vegetable oil

1) Insert toothpick under black vein of shrimps and remove. Remove shells. Cut off tip of tail and squeeze out water. Score the underside in three or four places.
2) For the horse mackerel, ask the fishmonger to prepare it for tempura.
3) Remove stems from Chinese black mushrooms and make a crosswise incision on the tops. Cut

Cal.	Time	Cost
64	C	B

38 · Broiled shrimps [*Ebi no onigara yaki* エビの鬼がら焼き]

INGREDIENTS

12 large shrimps (*ebi* エビ)
Marinade
    4 tbsps soy sauce
    1½ tbsps *mirin*

1) Bend shrimps slightly and insert toothpick under black vein and remove. Put shrimps with heads and shells into marinade and leave for 15 minutes. Drain.
2) Stick two metal skewers into each shrimp.
3) Boil the leftover sauce until it thickens. Broil shrimps over a broiling net until shells turn red. Remove skewers while shrimps are hot. Baste with leftover sauce.
4) Shrimps are to be served with heads and shells intact.

NOTE

• **For microwave cooking:** Cook for 2 minutes. After cooking brush with sauce.

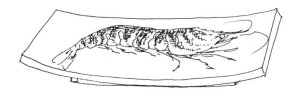

5

Egg and tofu

Although prices are high in Japan, some things such as eggs and tofu are cheap. Some say that Japanese cooking begins with sweet rolled egg (*tamago yaki*) and ends with rolled egg.

Tofu is made from soybeans and is noted as a health food due to its high protein and calcium content. It is delicious even when served uncooked with a dipping sauce and seasonings.

There are two types of tofu, *kinugoshi* and *momen*. *Kinugoshi* contains vitamin B and is very soft and somewhat difficult to handle, while on the other hand *momen* is firmer and easier to handle. Tofu is also made into various forms such as *abura age*, thin sheets that have been fried; *atsu age*, deep fried; *ganmodoki*, tofu mixed with vegetables and deep fried; and *kōyadōfu*, or *kōridōfu*, frozen and dried tofu.

(5)—EGG & TOFU

39·Rolled egg
[*Dashimaki tamago* だし巻き卵]

INGREDIENTS

6 eggs (*tamago* 卵)
6 tbsps water
¼ tbsp *dashinomoto*
½ tsp salt
1 tbsp sugar
4 tbsps vegetable oil
½ cup grated radish (*daikon oroshi* ダイコンおろし)

1) Beat 3 eggs lightly, add 3 tbsps water, 1/8 tsp *dashinomoto*, ¼ tsp salt and ½ tbsp sugar.

2) Heat small amount of oil in a square egg roll pan (*tamago yaki ki*). Pour in enough egg mixture to cover bottom of pan (illustration (a)). When egg begins to set, using a spatula, roll egg up and away from yourself toward opposite end of pan. Grease exposed bottom of pan with paper towel soaked in oil (b). Add more egg and repeat process, lifting cooked roll to allow uncooked egg to adhere to it (c). As egg begins to set, roll egg back in opposite direction (d). Continue in this manner until all egg is cooked and rolled. Wrap hot egg roll in a bamboo mat (*makisu*) to give it a good round shape. Cut roll into 3-cm-thick slices.

3) Peel and finely grate radish. Serve with egg roll.

• Sweet rolled egg (*tamago yaki*)

Mix together 6 eggs, 4 tbsps sugar, 2 tbsps sake, ½ tsp soy sauce and salt. Cook as in Step 2.

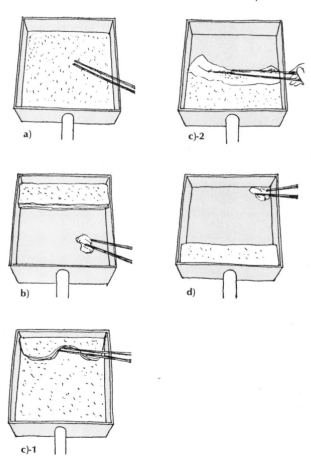

a)

c)-2

b)

d)

c)-1

40 · Egg custard with shrimps and vegetables
[*Chawan mushi* 茶わん蒸し]

INGREDIENTS

100 g chicken breasts (*tori muneniku* トリ胸肉)
4 Chinese black mushrooms (*shiitake* シイタケ)
8 shrimps (*ebi* エビ)
12 trefoil stalks (*mitsuba* ミツバ)
3 eggs (*tamago* 卵)
Broth
    2½ cups water
    ½ tsp *dashinomoto*
1 tsp soy sauce
pinch of salt

1) Add 2½ cups water to a pan with *dashinomoto*, soy sauce and a pinch of salt to make broth. Bring to the boil. Cool.
2) Slice chicken and sprinkle with 1 tsp soy sauce and 1 tsp sake.
3) Insert toothpick under black vein of shrimps and remove. Discard heads. Boil shrimps in salted water for 2 minutes. Cool and remove shells, leaving tails intact.
4) Remove stems from Chinese black mushrooms and slice. Cut trefoil into 5-cm lengths.
5) Beat eggs lightly and mix with broth then strain.
6) Place chicken, shrimps and Chinese black mushrooms in individual ovenproof serving cups with lids. Pour in egg mixture. (If serving cups with lids are not available, use tea cups and cover with

aluminum foil.

7) Preheat oven to 200° C. Place cups in large pan half filled with water. Steam for 20 minutes. When custard is set remove from oven and decorate with trefoil.

8) Serve hot with lids on.

NOTE

• Precooked carrot (*ninjin*) and bamboo shoots (*takenoko*) can be used.

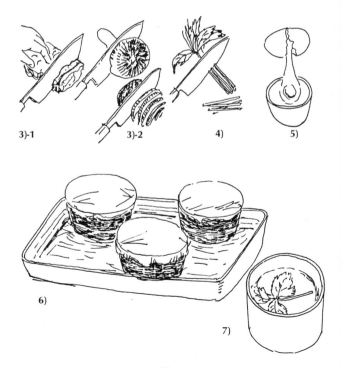

3)-1

3)-2

4)

5)

6)

7)

Cal.	Time	Cost
319	B	B

41 · Crab and vegetable omelet
[*Kanitama* カニ玉]

INGREDIENTS

1 small can of crab meat (*kani no kanzume* カニの缶詰)
6 eggs (*tamago* 卵)
½ long onion (*naganegi* 長ネギ)
2 Chinese black mushrooms (*shiitake* シイタケ)
½ cup boiled bamboo shoots* (*yude takenoko* ゆでタケノコ)
2 tbsps frozen green peas (*guriin piisu* グリーンピース)
1 tsp potato starch (*katakuriko* カタクリ粉) or cornstarch
Sauce

    3/4 cup water (with 1 tsp of instant chicken bouillon granules, optional)
    1½ tbsps soy sauce
    salt
    1½ tbsps sugar
    1 tsp potato starch
vegetable oil

1) Remove cartilage from crab meat.
2) Finely slice long onion. Cut Chinese black mushrooms and bamboo shoots into thin strips. Mix crab meat and vegetables except green peas with 1 tsp potato starch.
3) Beat eggs lightly and add crab meat and vegetable mixture. Season with salt and 1 tsp soy sauce. Mix well and divide into four portions.

4) In a frying pan heat 1 tbsp vegetable oil. Pour in one portion of egg mixture. When half cooked, turn over and cook other side. Mixture makes four omelets

5) Mix together ingredients for sauce and boil. Add potato starch (dissolved in 2 tbsps water) and green peas to mixture and stir until it thickens slightly. Pour sauce over omelets and serve.

* Boiled bamboo shoots are available at supermarkets.

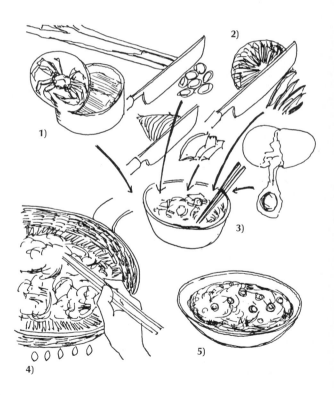

(5)—EGG & TOFU

42·Fresh tofu
[*Hiya-yakko* 冷奴]

INGREDIENTS

1 block tofu (豆腐)
2 slices ham (*hamu* ハム)
1-cm piece fresh ginger (*shōga* ショウガ)
½ long onion (*naganegi* 長ネギ)
1 tbsp sesame seeds (*iri goma* いりゴマ)
4 tbsps soy sauce

1) Cut ham and ginger into thin strips, finely slice long onion.
2) Cut tofu into quarters and place in small bowls. Top tofu with ham, ginger, long onion and sesame seeds. Serve with soy sauce.

NOTE

• Cold tofu is a refreshing food in the summer and is usually served with a dipping sauce. Heat 1 cup soy sauce, 1 tsp *dashinomoto* and 2 tbsps *mirin*. Cool and refrigerate, or use ready-made sauce for *hiya-yakko*. Top tofu with bonito flakes, grated ginger or sliced long onion. Also place tofu in refrigerator in water.

• In winter boil tofu (*yudōfu*) and serve with a dipping sauce. Boil 1 cup soy sauce, 1 tsp *dashinomoto* and 1 tbsp sake.

Cal.	Time	Cost
112	B	B

43·Tofu salad

[*Tōfu sarada* 豆腐サラダ]

INGREDIENTS

1 block tofu (豆腐)
1 cucumber (*kyūri* キュウリ)
2 medium-size tomatoes (*tomato* トマト)
1 egg (*tamago* 卵)
Dressing
     2⅔ tbsps soy sauce
     4 tsps lemon juice
     2 tsps sesame oil
     salt and pepper

1) Wrap tofu in kitchen paper or cloth and press between two plates for 15 minutes to remove excess liquid. Cut tofu into 3-cm cubes.
2) Slice cucumber. Cut tomatoes into segments.
3) Scramble egg.
4) Mix ingredients for dressing together and stir well.
5) Place tofu, vegetables and scrambled egg in a salad bowl. Pour over dressing.

NOTE

• Celery and lettuce can be added.
• Already prepared dressings can be used.

(5)—EGG & TOFU

44 · Tofu with vegetables
[*Iridōfu* 炒り豆腐]

INGREDIENTS

1½ blocks tofu (豆腐)
120 g minced chicken (*tori hikiniku* トリひき肉)
⅓ carrot (*ninjin* ニンジン)
4 Chinese black mushrooms (*shiitake* シイタケ)
⅓ cup snow peas (*sayaendō* サヤエンドウ)
1½ tbsps sesame oil
1½ tbsps soy sauce
1 tbsp *mirin*
1 tbsp sugar
salt

1) Wrap tofu in kitchen paper or cloth and press between two plates for 15 minutes to remove excess
   water.
2) Slice carrot and cut into quarters and boil for 5
   minutes. Remove stems from Chinese black
   mushrooms and cut mushrooms into quarters.
3) Remove ends from snow peas and boil in salted
   water for 3 minutes. Cut into 3-cm pieces.
4) Place tofu in a bowl and stir in with chopsticks.
5) Heat sesame oil in a pan. Sauté minced chicken,
   carrot and Chinese black mushrooms for 5
   minutes. Add tofu and season with soy sauce,
   mirin, sugar and salt. Stir well and simmer for 4
   minutes. Add snow peas and turn off heat.

1)

2)-1

2)-2

3)

4)

5)-1

5)-2

5)-3

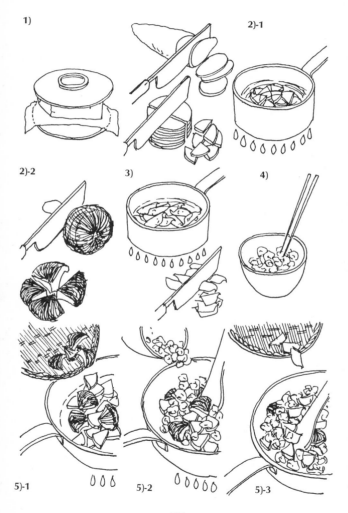

75

(5)—EGG & TOFU

45·Tofu steak
[*Tōfu sutēki* 豆腐ステーキ]

INGREDIENTS

2 blocks tofu (豆腐)
flour
2 tbsps vegetable oil
Sauce
    1 onion (*tamanegi* タマネギ)
    8 mushrooms (*masshurūmu* マッシュルーム)
    2 tbsps water
    2 tbsps soy sauce
    1 tbsp sake
    1 tbsp potato starch (*katakuriko* カタクリ粉) or
    cornstarch
    3 tbsps water
vegetable oil

1) Cut tofu in half horizontally. Wrap tofu in kitchen paper or cloth and press between two plates for 15 minutes to remove excess liquid. Season with salt and pepper and dust with flour.
2) Cut onion in half and slice. Slice mushrooms. Heat vegetable oil in a pan and add onion. Sauté until light brown and stir in mushrooms. Sauté for 30 seconds then add water, soy sauce and sake. Add potato starch mixed with water and stir until vegetable mixture thickens.
3) Heat 3 tbsps vegetable oil in a pan and sauté tofu on both sides until golden brown.
4) Serve tofu with sauce.

Cal.	Time	Cost
274	C	A

46·Fried tofu
[*Agedashi-dōfu* 揚げ出し豆腐]

INGREDIENTS

2 blocks tofu (豆腐)
potato starch (*katakuriko* カタクリ粉) or cornstarch
vegetable oil
¼ chives (*asatsuki* アサツキ)
½ cup bonito flakes (*katsuobushi* カツオブシ)
Sauce

     1 cup water
     ½ tsp *dashinomoto*
     ¼ cup *mirin*
     ½ cup soy sauce

1) Wrap tofu in kitchen paper or cloth and press between two plates for 15 minutes to remove excess water. Cut tofu into four pieces. Dust with potato starch.
2) In a frying pan heat oil to 180° C (see P. xvi) and fry tofu until golden brown.
3) Finely slice chives.
4) Mix together ingredients for sauce and heat.
5) Serve tofu in individual bowls topped with sliced chives and bonito flakes and sauce.

NOTE

• *Karaageko* (already seasoned flour) can be used.
• Ketchup or mayonnaise can replace the sauce.

6
Vegetables

Japanese use vegetables in a variety of ways, apart from the usual methods of cooking them, vegetables are used raw in vinegared dishes and pickled in various ways. Most vegetables are available throughout the year due to agricultural technology. But of course, vegetables ripened naturally and in season have the highest nutritional value.

Perilla (*shiso*), long onion (*naganegi*), and ginger (*shōga*) are generally used as condiments.

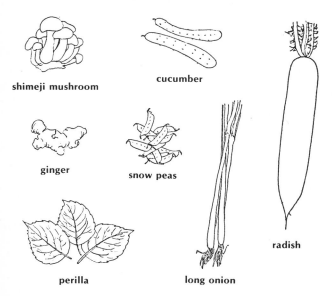

shimeji mushroom

cucumber

ginger

snow peas

perilla

long onion

radish

Chinese cabbage

horseradish

eggplant

Chinese black mushroom

dried black mushroom

citron

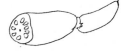

lotus root

taro

pumpkin

chive

Cal.	Time	Cost
11	B	A

47 · Cucumber and seaweed salad with vinegar dressing

[Kyūri to wakame no sunomono キュウリとワカメの酢の物]

INGREDIENTS

2 cucumbers (*kyūri* キュウリ)
⅓ cup seaweed (*nama wakame* 生ワカメ)
vinegar dressing
    3 tbsps rice vinegar
    1 tbsp soy sauce
    1 tbsp sugar
    salt

1) Cut ends off cucumbers. Slice cucumbers thinly sprinkle with salt and let stand for 10 minutes. Rinse cucumbers with water then squeeze to remove liquid.
2) Wash seaweed then soak in water for 5 minutes to remove salt. Drain and cut in 3-cm lengths.
3) Mix ingredients for vinegar dressing. Mix cucumber and seaweed together and pour over vinegar dressing just before serving.

NOTE

• Chicken breasts (*tori muneniku*) boiled and shredded; shrimps (*ebi*), boiled and shelled; bean sprouts (*moyashi*), string beans (*sayaingen*), asparagus (*asuparagasu*), celery (*serori*), radish (*daikon*) and carrot (*ninjin*) can be used instead.

- Soy sauce dressing
    - 2 tbsps rice vinegar
    - 1 tbsp soy sauce
    - 3 tbsps vegetable oil
    - salt and pepper
- Mayonnaise with sesame seeds
    - 4 tbsps mayonnaise
    - 2 tbsps white sesame seeds (*shirogoma*)
    - 1 tsp soy sauce

These dressings can be used with any type of salad, cooked meat or boiled fish.

Cal.	Time	Cost
62	B	A

48 · Spinach with sesame dressing [*Hōrensō no goma ae* ホウレンソウのゴマ和え]

INGREDIENTS

1 bunch spinach (*hōrensō* ホウレンソウ)
Sesame dressing
    3 tbsps ground sesame seeds (*suri goma* すりゴマ)
    1 tbsp soy sauce
    2 tbsps sugar

1) Cook spinach for 2 minutes in boiling water. Drain and rinse with cold water. Squeeze water out of spinach. Cut into 3-cm lengths.
2) Mix together ingredients for sesame dressing.
3) Just before serving, pour dressing over spinach and mix well.

NOTE

- Japanese green vegetable (*komatsuna*), chrysanthemum leaves (*shungiku*), bean sprouts (*moyashi*), string beans (*sayaingen*), or cabbage (*kyabetsu*) are suitable for this recipe.
- Sesame dressing can be substituted with instant *goma ae no moto* or peanut butter.
- If already ground sesame seeds are not available, grind roasted sesame seeds with mortar and pestle, or in a blender.
- **For microwave cooking:** Cook spinach covered for 1½ minutes.

Cal.	Time	Cost
30	B	A

49·Cabbage with mustard and soy sauce dressing
[*Kyabetsu no karashi-jōyu ae*
キャベツのカラシじょうゆ和え]

INGREDIENTS

5 cabbage leaves (*kyabetsu* キャベツ)
1/6 onion (*tamanegi* タマネギ)
Mustard and soy sauce dressing
　　½ tsp mustard (*karashi* カラシ)
　　2 tbsps soy sauce

1) Boil cabbage for 3 minutes. Drain and then cut into bite-size pieces.
2) Slice onion thinly and soak in water for 10 minutes. Squeeze out liquid.
3) Mix ingredients for dressing.
4) Mix cabbage and onion and pour dressing over vegetables just before serving.

NOTE

- Japanese green vegetable (*komatsuna*), asparagus (*asuparagasu*), or broccoli (*burokkori*) are also suitable.
- **For microwave cooking:** Cook cabbage covered for 1 minute.

Cal.	Time	Cost
29	C	A

50 · Marinated Chinese cabbage

[*Yude hakusai no su-abura-jōyu zuke* ゆでハクサイの酢油しょうゆ漬け]

INGREDIENTS

4 large Chinese cabbage leaves (*hakusai* ハクサイ)
1 tbsp chopped long onion (*naganegi* 長ネギ)
1 dried chili pepper (*aka tōgarashi* 赤トウガラシ)
1 tsp fresh ginger (*shōga* ショウガ)
Marinade
    2 tbsps soy sauce
    1½ tbsps rice vinegar
    1 tbsps vegetable oil
    ½ tbsp sesame oil

1) Separate Chinese cabbage leaves. Boil until soft and transparent. Drain. Squeeze lightly and cut into bite-size pieces.
2) Cut long onion and ginger into thin strips. Remove seeds from chili pepper and slice thinly.
3) Mix marinade ingredients, long onion, ginger and chili pepper well. Marinate Chinese cabbage for about 30 minutes, turning occasionally.
4) For a full flavor it is best to marinate cabbage overnight. Serve with any leftover marinade.

NOTE

• Cucumber (*kyūri*), or cabbage (*kyabetsu*) can be used instead. Cut and sprinkle with salt and let stand for 10 minutes. Squeeze out any liquid and marinate.

Cal.	Time	Cost
19	B	A

51·Sliced onion
[*Sarashi tamanegi* さらしタマネギ]

INGREDIENTS

1 onion (*tamanegi* タマネギ)
½ cup bonito flakes (*katsuobushi* カツオブシ)
soy sauce

1) Peel onion and cut in half. Slice thinly. Soak in water for 10 minutes and drain.
2) Squeeze water out of onion. Place bonito flakes on top of onion. Serve with soy sauce.

NOTE

- Any salad dressing, mayonnaise or Worcestershire sauce can be used.

Ready-made dressings

86

Cal.	Time	Cost
86	B	A

52·Sautéed burdock and carrot

[*Gobō to ninjin no kimpira* ゴボウ とニンジンのキンピラ]

INGREDIENTS

1 burdock stick (*gobō* ゴボウ)
¼ carrot (*ninjin* ニンジン)
2 tbsps sugar
1½ tbsps sake
3 tbsps soy sauce
2 tbsps sesame oil

1) Wash burdock and scrape off skin with the back of knife. Cut crosswise into 5-cm pieces and slice lengthwise then cut into thin strips. Soak in water with 1 tsp vinegar for 5 minutes. Peel carrot and cut in the same way.

2) Heat sesame oil in a pan. Sauté burdock and carrot until soft, then add sugar, sake and soy sauce. Cook over low heat, stirring until liquid has evaporated.

NOTE

• 2 dried chili peppers add a tang to this recipe. Trim ends, take out seeds and slice. Sauté with vegetables.

• 1 tbsp roasted white sesame seeds (*shiro goma*) can be added. Sprinkle over burdock and carrot just before turning off heat.

• Use radish (*daikon*) or carrot by itself.

Cal.	Time	Cost
103	B	A

53·Eggplant with *miso*
[*Nasu no dengaku miso ae* ナスの 田楽みそ和え]

INGREDIENTS

6 eggplants (*nasu* ナス)
vegetable oil
Miso sauce
    4 tbsps *miso*
    2½ tbsps sugar
    1 tbsp *mirin*

1) Cut off stems and tops of eggplant. Cut crosswise into 3-cm lengths. Soak in water for 5 minutes. Remove and dry with paper.
2) Heat oil in saucepan and sauté eggplant until brown and soft.
3) In a saucepan mix ingredients for *miso* sauce and boil until thick.
4) Place eggplant on individual serving plates and spread *miso* sauce on top.

NOTE

• Bonito flakes and soy sauce, *ponzu jōyu* (soy sauce and lemon juice), ketchup and Worcestershire sauce can replace *miso* sauce.

Cal.	Time	Cost
88	A	A

54·Eggplant and green pepper with *miso*

[*Nasu to piiman no miso itame* ナスとピーマンのみそ炒め]

INGREDIENTS

4 eggplants (*nasu* ナス)
3 green peppers (*piiman* ピーマン)
3 tbsps vegetable oil
1 tbsp *miso*
1 tbsp *mirin*

1) Cut eggplant horizontally into half, then into 3-cm lengths. Soak in water for 5 minutes.
2) Cut green peppers into half. Remove seeds and cut into bite-size pieces.
3) Mix *miso* and *mirin*.
4) Heat vegetable oil in a frying pan. Add eggplant and sauté for 3 minutes. Add green peppers and sauté until soft. Stir in *miso* mixture and sauté for 1 more minute.

NOTE

• Ketchup, Worcestershire sauce and canned meat sauce for spaghetti make interesting changes from *miso*.

Cal.	Time	Cost
151	C	A

55 · Sweet potato with lemon

[*Satsumaimo no remon ni* サツマイモのレモン煮]

INGREDIENTS

2 medium-size sweet potatoes (*satsumaimo* サツマイモ)
½ lemon (*remon* レモン)
4½ tbsps sugar
salt

1) Cut sweet potatoes crosswise into 1.5-cm widths. Peel and soak in water for 5 minutes.
2) Wash lemon and slice thinly.
3) Put 5 cups water and sweet potatoes in a pan and boil. After boiling for 1 minute, turn off heat and drain.
4) Place sweet potatoes in a pan and cover with water. Add sugar and salt. Top with lemon. Cover with aluminum foil and boil on medium heat until broth is reduced by one-third.
5) Remove lemon slices. Serve sweet potatoes.

NOTE

• **For microwave cooking:** Place sweet potatoes (cut and peeled), lemon, ½ cup water, 4½ tbsps sugar and a pinch of salt in a bowl. Cover with plastic wrap and make a hole in the center then cover with one more sheet of plastic wrap. Cook for 8 minutes.

Cal.	Time	Cost
304	B	B

56·Potato with minced beef sauce
[*Jagaimo ankake* ジャガイモあんかけ]

INGREDIENTS

3 or 4 potatoes (*jagaimo* ジャガイモ)
200 g minced beef (*gyū hikiniku* 牛ひき肉)
3 tbsps sake
3 tbsps sugar
4 tbsps soy sauce
1 tbsp potato starch (*katakuriko* カタクリ粉)
or cornstarch
3 tbsps water

1) Peel and cut potatoes into four or six pieces and soak in water for 2 minutes. Boil potatoes in salted water until soft. Drain.
2) Mix sake, sugar and soy sauce in a pan, boil and add minced beef. Simmer for 5 minutes and thicken with potato starch mixed with water.
3) Pour minced beef sauce over potatoes.

NOTE

• Taro (*satoimo*), or pumpkin (*kabocha*) can be substituted.

Cal.	Time	Cost
157	D	B

57 · Soybeans with vegetables
[*Gomoku mame* 五目豆]

INGREDIENTS

½ cup soybeans (*daizu* 大豆)
10-cm piece of dried kelp (*kombu* コンブ)
⅔ burdock stick (*gobō* ゴボウ)
⅔ cup lotus root (*renkon* レンコン)
¼ carrot (*ninjin* ニンジン)
½ block *konnyaku* (コンニャク)
½ cup sugar
2 tbsps soy sauce

1) Wash soybeans and soak in 3 cups of water overnight.
2) Wipe kelp with a cloth and cut with scissors into ½-cm pieces. Soak in 1 cup water for 30 minutes. Retain this water for future use.
3) Scrape skin off burdock and cut into rounds. Soak in water with 1 tbsp rice vinegar for 5 minutes.
4) Slice lotus root into 0.8-cm rings and then cut into quarters. Soak in water for 5 minutes.
5) Cut carrot into 0.8-cm pieces. Boil *konnyaku* for 2 minutes and cut into 1-cm cubes.
6) Boil soybeans in the water they were soaked in plus the water from the kelp. When beans reach the boil turn down heat and simmer for 1 hour. Or until beans are soft.
7) Add other vegetables, kelp and simmer until cooked. Add sugar, simmer for 5 minutes. Add soy sauce, simmer for 1 minute and turn off heat.

- Any beans can be used instead of soybeans.
- Canned soybeans can be used to save preparation time.

Bean sprouts and green pepper salad with curry dressing [*Moyashi to piiman no karēzu ae*]

3 cups bean sprouts (*moyashi* もやし)
4 green peppers (*piiman* ピーマン)
Curry dressing
    3 tbsps rice vinegar
    1 tsp curry powder
    ½ tbsp soy sauce
    ½ tsp sugar
    salt

1) Boil bean sprouts for 3 minutes and drain.
2) Cut green peppers into halves. Remove seeds and shred. Boil green peppers for 2 minutes. Put in cold water to cool and drain.
3) Mix ingredients for curry dressing.
4) Mix bean sprouts and green peppers. Pour over curry dressing just over them before eating.

7

One-pot dishes

This type of cooking is very popular in winter as it creates a cosy atmosphere, with family members or guests sitting around the table helping themselves to the food as it cooks in an earthenware pot in front of them.

When doing this type of cooking parboil any vegetables that take time to cook.

If a portable burner is not available any of the dishes in this section can be cooked on a regular stove and the pot transferred to the table. Some recipes using a hot plate are included in this section.

58 · Sukiyaki
[スキ焼き]

INGREDIENTS

600 g thinly sliced beef (*gyū sukiyakiyō* 牛スキ焼き用)
4 long onions (*naganegi* 長ネギ)
1 bunch chrysanthemum leaves (*shungiku* シュンギク)
8 Chinese black mushrooms (*shiitake* シイタケ)
1 pack *shirataki*
1 block broiled tofu (*yakidōfu* 焼き豆腐)
8 wheat gluten cakes (*yakifu* 焼きふ)
4 eggs (*tamago* 卵)
Warishita stock
    1 cup water
    ½ cup soy sauce
    ½ cup *mirin*
    3 tbsps sugar
vegetable oil or suet (*gyū aburami* 牛アブラ身)

1) Cut long onion diagonally (see P. 128 H). Cut chrysanthemum leaves in half. Remove stems from Chinese black mushrooms and make crosswise incisions on tops.
2) Blanch *shirataki*. Drain and cut into 10-cm lengths. Cut broiled tofu into 1-cm cubes. Soak wheat gluten cake in water until soft. Squeeze out liquid.
3) Mix water, soy sauce, *mirin* and sugar to make *warishita* stock.
4) Break eggs into individual serving bowls and beat lightly.
5) Grease a pan with suet or oil and heat on a por-

table burner on the table until suet is half melted.
6) Sauté some of the beef, add small portions of the other ingredients then add *warishita* stock.
7) When cooked, guests serve themselves. Dip the hot food into the raw egg and eat. If stock becomes too strong add boiling water.

NOTE

• Ready-made *warishita* stock is available at supermarkets.

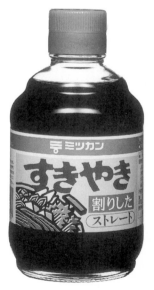

Ready-made *warishita* stock

Cal.	Time	Cost
764	C	D

59 · *Shabushabu*

[　シャブシャブ　]

---

600 g thinly sliced beef (*gyū shabushabu yō*　牛シャブシャブ用)

10-cm piece of dried kelp (*kombu*　コンブ) or 1 tsp *dashinomoto*

4 Chinese cabbage leaves (*hakusai*　ハクサイ)

½ bunch chrysanthemum leaves (*shungiku* シュンギク)

2 long onions (*naganegi*　長ネギ)

8 Chinese black mushrooms (*shiitake* シイタケ)

1 pack *shirataki*

Sesame seed sauce (*goma dare*　ゴマだれ)

> 6 tbsps ground white sesame seeds (*suri goma* すりゴマ
>
> 1 clove garlic
>
> 1 tbsp white *miso*
>
> 2 tbsps soy sauce
>
> 1 tbsp *mirin*
>
> 1 tbsp sake
>
> ½ cup water
>
> 1 tbsp rice vinegar

Ponzu jōyu

> 3 tbsps lemon juice
>
> ½ cup soy sauce

Condiments

Goma dare and **ponzu jōyu**

> ½ cup grated radish (*daikon oroshi* ダイコンおろし)
>
> 2 chives (*asatsuki* アサツキ) finely chopped
>
> 1 tbsp grated fresh ginger (*oroshi shōga* ダイコンおろし)

1) Soak dried kelp in 6 cups water for 40 minutes.

2) Fold sliced beef in two and arrange on a platter.
3) Cut chrysanthemum leaves in half.
4) Cut long onions into 4-cm lengths. Cut Chinese cabbage into bite-size pieces. Remove stems from Chinese black mushrooms.
5) Tie *shirataki* into small bundles and blanch.
6) Put all the vegetables on a platter.
7) Crush garlic. Mix together ingredients to make sesame sauce and *ponzu joyu*.
8) Prepare condiments.
9) Place dried kelp and the water in which it was soaked in a shallow pan on a portable burner on the table.
10) Put beef into boiling water using chopsticks. Leave for several seconds until meat changes color. Remove and dip into sauce, eat with condiments. Skim off any scum. Add small amounts of vegetables to stock. Diners serve themselves from the pan. Be careful not to add too many ingredients at one time.

| NOTE |

• Ready-made *goma dare* and *ponzu jōyu* are available at supermarkets.

Cal.	Time	Cost
296	B	D

60·Chicken, seafood and vegetables
[*Yosenabe*   よせ鍋]

INGREDIENTS

300 g chicken thighs (*tori momoniku*   トリもも肉)
300 g cod (*tara* タラ)
8 clams (*hamaguri*   ハマグリ)
4 large shrimps (*ebi* エビ)
1 block tofu (豆腐)
½ bunch chrysanthemum leaves (*shungiku* シュンギク)
6 Chinese cabbage leaves (*hakusai* ハクサイ)
Broth
     6 cups water
     1 tsp *dashinomoto*
     4 tbsps soy sauce
     2 tbsps *mirin*
     2 tbsps sake
Dipping sauce (*ponzu jōyu*   ポン酢じょうゆ)
     3 tbsps lemon juice
     ½ cup soy sauce
Condiments
     1 cup grated radish (*daikon oroshi* ダイコンおろし)

1) Cut chicken into 3-cm pieces.
2) Cut fish into 6-cm pieces.
3) Put toothpick under black vein of shrimps and remove the vein. Remove shells.
4) Soak clams in 5 cups water with 5 tsps salt for 4 hours to remove sand.
5) Cut tofu into 8 pieces.
6) Cut chrysanthemum leaves in half.

7) Cut Chinese cabbage into bite-size pieces.
8) Arrange vegetables, chicken, fish, clams and shrimps on a platter.
9) Mix ingredients for dipping sauce, and pour into individual serving bowls.
10) Mix ingredients for broth.
11) Place some of the chicken, seafood and vegetables in a shallow pot on a portable gas or electric burner on the table. Pour in enough broth to cover ingredients.
12) Boil and skim off any scum that forms. When everything is cooked, add chrysanthemum leaves.
13) Diners serve themselves. Dip ingredients into sauce with condiments.

NOTE

• Chicken on the bone is also suitable for this recipe. Long onion (*naganegi*) and carrot (*ninjin*) can be used. Instant *ponzu jōyu* is available at super-markets.

Instant *ponzu jōyu*

101

Cal.	Time	Cost
436	C	B

61·Fish cake potpourri
[*Oden* おでん]

INGREDIENTS

¼ radish (*daikon* ダイコン)
1 block *konnyaku* (コンニャク)
4 deep fried tofu and vegetable cakes (*ganmodoki* ガンモドキ)
2 fish cakes (*chikuwa* チクワ)
8 fish cake balls (*age bōru* 揚げボール)
8 taros (*satoimo* サトイモ)
8 quail's eggs (*uzura no tamago* ウズラの卵)
15-cm piece of dried kelp (*kombu* コンブ)
Broth
    6 cups water
    ½ cup sake
    3 tbsps *mirin*
    1 tbsp sugar
    1 tsp salt
    3 tbsps soy sauce
mustard

1) Peel radish and cut crosswise into 2-cm lengths and boil until soft.
2) Peel taros and boil until soft.
3) Cut *konnyaku* into bite-size pieces and blanch.
4) Boil quail's eggs and shell. Cut *chikuwa* into 5-cm lengths.
5) Put water enough to cover fish cakes, kelp and other ingredients for broth an earthen ware pot. Bring broth to the boil, add vegetables and other ingredients. Simmer for 1 hour over low heat.

Place earthenware pot on a portable burner on the table and cook.

6) Diners serve themselves. Serve *oden* with mustard.

NOTE

• Fish cake, such as *age bōru*, *satsuma age*, *gobōmaki* and *hampen* can be added. *Oden* sets are sold at supermarkets, and *age* shops have a wide range of foods for *oden*.

Instant *oden* broth

62 · Barbecued meat, seafood and vegetables
[*Teppanyaki* 鉄板焼き   ]

INGREDIENTS

600 g beef, pork or chicken (*gyūniku,* 牛肉   *butaniku*
ブタ肉   or *toriniku* トリ肉)
8 shrimps (*ebi* エビ)
1 onion (*tamanegi* タマネギ)
1 green pepper (*piiman* ピーマン)
8 Chinese black mushrooms (*shiitake* シイタケ)
⅓ carrot (*ninjin* ニンジン)
1 potato (*jagaimo* ジャガイモ)
vegetable oil
Barbecue sauce
     ½ cup ketchup
     ¼ cup Worcestershire sauce
Sesame seed sauce (*goma dare* ゴマだれ)
     6 tbsps white sesame seeds (*shiro goma* 白ゴマ)
     ½ cup water
     1 tbsp white *miso*
     1 tbsp *mirin*
     1 tbsp sake
     2 tsps soy sauce
     1 tbsp rice vinegar
     1 clove garlic crushed (*nin-niku* ニンニク)

1) Cut meat into bite-size pieces.
2) Shell shrimps leaving tails intact. Insert toothpick
    under black vein of shrimps and remove vein.
3) Slice onion into 0.5-cm rings. Cut green pepper in-
    to bite-size pieces. Remove stems from mush-

rooms.

4) Peel carrot and potato and cut into rounds and parboil.

5) Make sauces.

6) Heat hot plate on table and grease. Place meat, seafood and vegetables on hot plate and cook.

7) Diners serve themselves. Dip food into sauces of your choice.

NOTE

- Cabbage (*kyabetsu*), bean sprouts (*moyashi*), long onion (*naganegi*) and clams (*hamaguri*) can also be used.
- *Ponzu jōyu* is a tasty sauce for this dish.
- Ready-made barbecue sauce, sesame seed sauce and *ponzu jōyu* are available at supermarkets.

Ready-made sauce

Cal.	Time	Cost
330	B	B

63·Pancake with meat and vegetables
[*Okonomiyaki* お好み焼き]

INGREDIENTS

Batter
  2 cups flour
  1½ cups water
  1 egg (*tamago* 卵) lightly beaten
  salt and pepper
4 cabbage leaves (*kyabetsu* キャベツ)
100 g sliced pork (*buta usugiri niku* ブタ薄切り肉)
vegetable oil
Sauce
  3 tbsps Worcestershire sauce
  1 tbsp ketchup
Mayonnaise sauce
  3 tbsps soy sauce
  1 tbsp mayonnaise
Condiments
  bonito flakes (*katsuobushi* カツオブシ)
  red pickled ginger (*beni shōga* 紅ショウガ)
  dried seaweed (*ao nori* 青ノリ)

1) Mix ingredients for batter.

2) Remove hard part of cabbage and slice finely. Cut pork into strips. Add cabbage and pork to batter.

3) Heat vegetable oil in a skillet. Pour enough batter mixture to cover skillet and cook. When bubbles form, turn over and cook until light brown. Mix sauce ingredients together and brush sauce over one side of pancake and remove from skillet. Sprinkle any of the condiments over pancake.

8

Noodles

There are two types of Japanese noodles; buckwheat noodles (*soba*) and wheat noodles (*udon*). Both of these noodles are available precooked or dried. Dried noodles should be boiled for about 10 minutes, then rinsed with water. The precooked variety is just added to a hot soup.

Sōmen and *hiyamugi* are wheat noodles. *Sōmen* is very fine and *hiyamugi* is a little thicker. Both of these noodles, are eaten in the summer and served cold with a dipping sauce, usually accompanied with chopped perilla (*shiso*), grated ginger (*shōga*), or chopped spring onions.

Chinese noodles (*chūkasoba*) are quite popular among Japanese. These noodles are usually precooked and can be used in a variety of ways.

	Cal.	Time	Cost
	442	A	A

64 · Handmade wheat noodles
[*Teuchi udon* 手打ちウドン]

INGREDIENTS

2½ cups bread flour (*kyōryokuko* 強力粉)
2 cups cake flour (*hakurikiko* 薄力粉)
200～250 ml water
1 tsp salt
Potato starch (*katakuriko* カタクリ粉)
Soup
    ½ cup *mentsuyu** (めんつゆ)
    2 tbsps chopped long onion (*naganegi* 長ネギ)

1) Put flour, water and salt in a bowl and mix into a dough.
2) Knead dough until soft and pliable.
3) Sprinkle potato starch over table, roll dough out with a rolling pin to 0.5-cm thick.
4) Cut dough (see illustration) to make noodles.
5) Heat water in a large saucepan, add noodles and boil for 5 minutes. Drain.
6) Place noodles into individual bowls. Add ½ cup water to *mentsuyu* and boil for 1 minute to make soup. Place chopped long onion over soup. Dip noodles into soup.

* *mentsuyu* is an instant soup for noodles.

Hot soup for wheat and buckwheat noodles
2 cups *mirin*
2 cups soy sauce
3 tbsps sugar

2 cups dried bonito flakes (*katsuobushi* カツオブシ)

1) Put *mirin* in a pan and boil for 1 minute. Add soy sauce and sugar, skim off any scum. Add dried bonito flakes and boil for 1 minute more over a medium heat. Turn off heat and strain.
2) This soup is concentrated and needs to be diluted with water. Boil and pour over cooked noodles.

Cold soup for wheat and buckweat noodles (*mentsuyu*)

½ cup *mirin*
1½ tbsps sugar
2¼ cups water
½ cup soy sauce
1 cup dried bonito flakes

1) Put *mirin* and sugar in a pan and boil for 1 minute.
2) Add water, soy sauce, bonito flakes and boil over a medium heat for 1 minute. Turn off heat, strain and refrigerate.

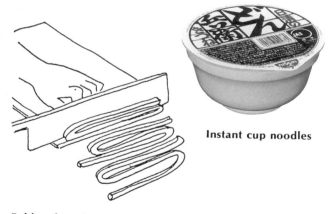

Instant cup noodles

Fold and cut into 0.3-mm-wide strips.

Cal.	Time	Cost
381	B	A

65 · Noodles with chicken and vegetables
[*Tori nanban* トリ南ばん]

***

INGREDIENTS

4 packs boiled wheat noodles (*yude udon*　ゆでウドン)
120 g chicken breasts (*tori muneniku* トリ胸肉)
¼ small carrot (*ninjin* ニンジン)
4 Chinese black mushrooms (*shiitake* シイタケ)
½ bunch spinach (*hōrenso* ホウレンソウ)
1 long onion (*naganegi* 長ネギ)
Soup
    6 cups water
    2 tsps *dashinomoto*
    4 tbsps *mirin*
    6 tbsp soy sauce
Condiments
    1 long onion (*naganegi* 長ネギ)
    powdered red pepper and spices (*shichimi tō-garashi* 七味トウガラシ)

1) Cut chicken into 3-cm cubes and season with salt and sake and let stand for 10 minutes.
2) Slice carrots and then cut slices into quarter.
3) Remove stems from mushrooms. Make a crisscross incision on the tops.
4) Cut long onion diagonally (see P. 128 H).
5) Thinly slice long onion to use as a condiment. Soak in water for 10 minutes and drain.
6) Bring 2 cups water to the boil, add chicken and boil for 5 minutes. Add long onion and boil for a minute and drain. Add 1 tsp soy sauce and 1 tsp

sugar to the leftover broth. Add carrots to the broth and cook for 3 minutes, add mushrooms and simmer until most of the liquid has evaporated. Drain.

7) Cook spinach in boiling water for 1 minute then drain. Rinse under running water and squeeze. Cut into 3-cm lengths.

8) Put ingredients for soup into a saucepan and boil. Add boiled noodles and cook for 1 minute. Pour soup and noodles into individual large rice bowls (*donburi*). Arrange chicken and vegetables on top of noodles. Add condiments.

NOTE

- Buckwheat noodles (*soba*) can be substituted for wheat noodles (*udon*).
- 2 pieces of deep fried tofu (*abura age*) can be added. Cook in ½ cup water, 1 tbsp soy sauce, 1 tbsp *mirin* and 1 tbsp sugar until liquid has nearly evaporated.
- Boiled fish cake (*kamaboko*)
- Instant soup for noodles (*mentsuyu*) can be used. Most of these soups are concentrates and need to be diluted.
- Curry soup is a tasty change. 5 cups water and ½ packet of curry roux. Boil water then mix in curry roux. Stir until it thickens slightly.

Cal.	Time	Cost
582	C	C

66 · Cold wheat noodles
[*Sōmen* ソーメン]

INGREDIENTS

400 g thin wheat noodles (*sōmen* ソーメン)
150 g chicken breasts (*tori muneniku* トリ胸肉)
3 dried Chinese black mushrooms (*shiitake* シイタケ)
1 cucumber (*kyūri* キュウリ)
2 eggs (*tamago* 卵)
8 shrimps (*ebi* エビ)
Sauce
    2 cups water
    1 tsp *dashinomoto*
    ½ cup soy sauce
    ⅓ cup *mirin*
Condiments
    ½ long onion (*naganegi* 長ネギ)
    5 pieces perilla (*shiso* シソ)

1) Boil ingredients for sauce. After boiling, simmer for 5 minutes. Cool.

2) Sprinkle salt, sake and potato starch over chicken. Boil water, add chicken and simmer for 5 minutes. Drain chicken and shred.

3) Cut cucumber into thin strips. Chop perilla and long onion. Soak sliced long onion in cold water for 5 minutes.

4) Soak dried Chinese black mushrooms in 1 cup water with 1 tsp sugar, until soft. Cut into 5-mm strips. Boil mushrooms in the water they were soaked in with 1½ tbsps soy sauce, 1½ tbsps sugar and 1 tbsp *mirin*, until water has almost evaporated.

5) Beat 2 eggs with a pinch of salt. Heat oil in a pan and pour enough egg mixture to thinly cover the pan. Cook for 30 seconds and turn over. Continue making the thin omelets until all egg mixture is used. Cut egg sheets into thin strips.

6) Boil ¼ cup water and add 8 shrimps with 2 tbsps sake and ½ tsp salt. Simmer until shrimps turn red. Drain and shell.

7) Boil water in a large saucepan. Add thin wheat noodles and stir. When noodles are boiling well, add ½ cup cold water. When it reaches boiling point again, boil for 2 minutes then turn off heat. Drain noodles and rinse in running cold water to remove starch.

8) Arrange noodles and other ingredients on a bamboo sieve or a platter. Pour sauce into individual serving bowls. Diners serve themselves with the noodles, chicken, egg and prawns. Dip in the sauce (add condiments to sauce beforehand) then eat together.

| NOTE |

• Ready-made sauce for *sōmen* (*somen no tsuyu*) is available at supermarkets.

(8)—NOODLES

67 · Noodles with tomato
[*Udon no tomato nikomi*
ウドンのトマト煮込み]

INGREDIENTS

4 packs precooked white wheat noodles (*yude udon* ゆでウドン)
2 tomatoes (*tomato* トマト)
1 carrot (*ninjin* ニンジン
4 slices ham (*hamu* ハム)
1 onion (*tamanegi* タマネギ)
2 green peppers (*piiman* ピーマン)
2 tbsps butter
salt and pepper
4 tbsps mayonnaise

1) Peel tomatoes, cut in half and take out seeds. Slice into 1-cm strips.
2) Cut carrot, ham, onion, and green pepper into 1-cm cubes.
3) Heat a saucepan and grease with butter, sauté carrot, ham, onion and green pepper. Add tomatoes at the end of cooking time. Season with salt and pepper. Add wheat noodles, mix well and turn off heat. Stir in mayonnaise.

NOTE

• Frozen mixed vegetables can be used instead of fresh vegetables.

Cal.	Time	Cost
843	B	B

68·Chinese noodles
[*Rāmen* ラーメン]

INGREDIENTS

4 packs Chinese noodles (*rāmen* ラーメン)
¼ bunch spinach (*hōrensō* ホウレンソウ)
8 slices roast pork* (*yakibuta* 焼きブタ)
⅓ long onion (*naganegi* 長ネギ)
Soup
    6 cups water
    2 chicken stock cubes
    2 tbsps sake
    1-cm piece of fresh ginger (*shōga* ショウガ)
    green part of 2 long onions (*naganegi* 長ネギ)
Spice (enough for one serving)
    ¼ tsp salt
    ½ tbsp soy sauce
    1 tsp lard or sesame oil

1) Slice ginger, cut green section of long onion into halves. Boil water, chicken stock cubes, sake, ginger and green onion. Keep on a rolling boil for 5 minutes then strain.
2) Blanch spinach and drain. Squeeze out excess water and cut into 5-cm lengths. Slice long onion thinly.
3) Add spice to individual large rice bowls (*donburi*).
4) Boil Chinese noodles for 3 minutes and drain.
5) Pour soup into the bowls with the spice. Add noodles to soup and top with roast pork, spinach, and long onion.
* Already cooked roast pork is available.

- Carrot (*ninjin*), cabbage (*kyabetsu*), bean sprouts (*moyashi*), onion (*tamanegi*), green pepper (*piiman*), Chinese black mushrooms (*shiitake*), snow peas (*sayaendo*), Chinese bamboo shoot (*menma*), sliced beef can be substituted.
- Vegetable oil can be used.

Various precooked Chinese noodles (instant *rāmen*) are sold in supermarkets.

* **Dry-type noodles:** Bring 1½ cups water to the boil. Add pack of noodles and boil for 3 minutes. Turn off heat and add powdered soup mix and stir.

* **Soft-type noodles:** Bring water to the boil and cook 1 pack of noodles for 3 minutes. Drain. In another saucepan boil 1½ cups of water, stir in soup essence and turn off heat. Pour soup into large rice bowls (*donburi*). Add cooked noodles to soup. (These noodles are usually kept in the refrigerator section in the supermarket).

* **Cup noodles:** Pour boiling water into instant cup noodles and powdered soup. When noodles are soft they are ready to eat.

Dry-type noodle   **Cup noodle**

Cal.	Time	Cost
639	B	B

69·Cold Chinese noodles
[*Hiyashi chūka*　冷やし中華　]

INGREDIENTS

4 packs Chinese noodles (*nama chūka men* なま中華めん)
1 tomato (*tomato* トマト)
1 cucumber (*kyūri* キュウリ)
1 cup bean sprouts (*moyashi* モヤシ)
100 g ham (*hamu* ハム)
2 eggs (*tamago* 卵)
Sauce
　　6 tbsps rice vinegar
　　3 tbsps soy sauce
　　2 tbsps sugar
　　4 tbsps water
　　2 tsps mustard
　　2 tbsps sesame oil

1) Boil Chinese noodles for 3 minutes then drain. Pour sesame oil over noodles, leave to cool.
2) Cut tomato, cucumber, and ham into fine strips. Blanch bean sprouts.
3) Cook thin omelets with a pinch of salt and cut into fine strips.
4) Mix together ingredients for sauce.
5) Place cold Chinese noodles in individual soup bowls and arrange vegetables, ham and egg on top. Season with sauce.

NOTE

• Ready-made sauce for *hiyashi chūka* is sold in supermarkets.
• Instant *hiyashi chūka* with sauce is available.

70 · Fried Chinese noodles with meat, vegetables
[*Yakisoba* 焼きソバ]

INGREDIENTS

4 packs Chinese noodles for frying (*yakisoba* 焼きソバ)
100 g sliced pork (*buta usugiri niku* ブタ薄切り肉)
3 cabbage leaves (*kyabetsu* キャベツ)
6 tbsps Worcestershire sauce
1 tbsp soy sauce
salt and pepper
vegetable oil
Condiments
    red pickled ginger (*beni shōga* 紅ショウガ)
    dried green seaweed (*ao nori* 青ノリ)

1) Cut pork into strips.
2) Remove hard part of cabbage and cut into thin strips.
3) Sauté cabbage and pork in a skillet for 3 minutes. Add noodles and 2 tbsps water, sauté for 1 minute, then stir in Worcestershire sauce and season with salt and pepper. Sauté for 1 minute more, then turn off heat. Sprinkle condiments on noodles before serving.

NOTE

- Bean sprouts (*moyashi*), carrots (*ninjin*), onions (*tamanegi*) can be used instead.
- Instant *yakisoba* packs (noodles and sauce) are also available.

9
Teas, drinks & sweets

To Japanese, tea means Japanese tea (*ocha*). Tea is always served after a meal. The way to make Japanese tea is almost the same as in the West, except the temperature of the water differs depending on the type of tea.

Sake, a rice wine is made by fermentation and differs in the degree of sweetness. Sake that is sweetish is call *amakuchi* and not so sweet sake is called *karakuchi*.

Cakes are not usually served as a dessert and are reserved for serving with tea. Japanese desserts mainly consist of red beans (*azuki*); it is served with either fruits or rice cakes.

71·Japanese teas

(1) Ordinary green tea (*sencha* 煎茶)

2 tbsps tea leaves
400 ml water
Put leaves into a teapot. Boil water for 3
minutes to remove chemical elements.
Wait until water is 80° C. Pour hot water
over tea leaves and let stand for 1 minute.
Pour tea into warmed tea cups. Tea bags
can be used.

(2) Roasted brown tea with a rich aroma (*hōjicha* ほうじ茶)

3 tbsps tea leaves
400 ml water
Put tea leaves into a teapot. Boil water for
3 minutes. Pour boiling water over tea
leaves. Pour tea into warmed tea cups.
Tea bags can be used.

(3) Unpolished rice tea (*genmaicha* 玄米茶)

3 tbsps tea leaves and grains
400 ml water
Follow steps for roasted brown tea
(*hōjicha*)

(4) Roasted barley tea (*mugicha* 麦茶)

Tea bags are commonly used for barley
tea. Infuse 1 tea bag in 1 liter of water for
30 minutes. In summer refrigerate it and
serve cold.

72·Sake (rice wine)

Hot sake (*atsukan* 熱かん)

Pour sake into sake container (sake *tokkuri*). In a small pan bring water to the boil, place *tokkuri* in the pan and boil for 2 or 3 minutes.
For microwave cooking: Heat sake in container for 1 mimute.

Shōchū (焼酎)

Japanese spirits distilled from rice, barley, millet, potato or sweet potato. Mix with cold or hot water, juice or soda.

Ume wine (*ume shu* 梅酒)

500 g fresh Japanese plums (*ao ume* 青梅)
200 g rock sugar (*kōri zatō* 氷砂糖)
900 ml *shōchū* (焼酎)

1) Rinse Japanese plums with water, remove calyx with toothpick then drain.
2) Place plums and rock sugar alternately in a large bottle and pour over *shōchū*.
3) Cover the bottle with a lid and keep in a dark, cool place for 3 months.
4) When the plums settle on the bottom of the jar and the liquor turns amber the wine is ready to drink. Ume wine can be mixed with cold or hot water, ice and soda water, or drink it straight.

• Fresh Japanese plums are available mainly in June.

Cal.	Time	Cost
322	B	B

73 · Azuki-bean soup with rice cakes
[*Oshiruko* おしるこ]

INGREDIENTS

200 g can azuki beans, or paste (*yude azuki no kan-zume* ゆでアズキの缶詰)
1 cup sugar
4 rice cake blocks (*mochi* モチ)

1) Toast rice cakes in a toaster or under the grill until soft. Soak in boiled water for 1 minute then drain.
2) In a saucepan bring 4 cups water to the boil, stir in azuki beans and sugar. Cook and stir until beans resemble thick soup.
3) Place rice cakes in a bowl and pour over bean mixture.

NOTE

Another way to eat rice cakes
- **Abekawa mochi:** Follow Step 1 of above recipe. Coat rice cakes with mixture of 2 tbsps soybean flour (*kinako*) and 2 tbsps sugar.
- **Isobe maki:** Toast rice cakes until soft. Dip in soy sauce and wrap with seaweed (*nori*).

Cal.	Time	Cost
194	C	D

74·Fruit in syrup with red beans and jelly cubes
[*Mitsumame* みつ豆]

INGREDIENTS

1 tsp powder agaragar (*kanten* 寒天)

2½ cups water

¾ cup mandarin oranges, canned (*mikan no kanzume* ミカンの缶詰)

1 whole peach, canned (*momo no kanzume* 桃の缶詰)

8 cherries, canned (*sakurambo no kanzume* サクランボの缶詰)

⅓ cup *azuki* beans, canned (*yude azuki no kanzume* ゆでアズキの缶詰)

Syrup

    1 cup sugar

    1 cup water

1) Boil the water and agaragar and keep on a rolling boil for 3 minutes. Strain, then pour into a mold and let it cool. Cut into 1-cm cubes.

2) In a saucepan boil 1 cup sugar and 1 cup water until the quantity is reduced by half then let it cool.

3) Drain canned fruit and *azuki* beans. Place fruit and agaragar jelly into small bowls and pour over syrup.

NOTE

• Any boiled beans in syrup are suitable.

• Fresh fruits such as apple, grapefruit, kiwi fruit, and pineapple can be used instead of canned fruits.

(9)— TEAS, DRINKS & SWEETS

75 · Fluffy snow jelly
[*Awayukikan* 淡雪かん]

INGREDIENTS

2 tbsps powdered agaragar (*kanten* 寒天)
2½ cups water
2 cups sugar
4 egg whites (*tamago no shiromi* 卵の白味)
½ tsp grated lemon rind
1 tbsp lemon juice

1) Put agaragar and sugar into 2½ cups water, bring to the boil then reduce heat and simmer for 3 minutes until sugar is dissolved. Let cool to room temperature.

2) Beat egg whites until stiff, add lemon rind and lemon juice, and fold slowly into agaragar. Mix well and leave until mixture begins to thicken, then pour into a wet or lightly greased 18-cm-square mold. Refrigerate until set. Take agaragar mixture out of the mold and cut into 8 pieces.

NOTE

• 1 tbsp orange liqueur can be added to enhance the flavor.

Cal.	Time	Cost
143	C	B

76·Sweet potato cake with chestnuts
[*Kuri kanoko* 栗かのこ　]

---

4 boiled chestnuts in syrup (*kuri no kanroni* 栗の甘露煮)
2 tbsps canned *azuki* beans (*yude azuki no kanzume* ゆでアズキの缶詰)
½ tsp powder agaragar (*kanten* 寒天)
6 tbsps water
1 sweet potato (*satsumaimo* サツマイモ)
pudding molds

1) Drain chestnuts and reserve syrup.
2) Peel sweet potato and cut into 1-cm thick slices. Boil sweet potato in water until soft then mash. Pour 1 tbsp chestnut syrup into sweet potato and roll into 4 balls.
3) Push chestnuts into each sweet potato ball and cover with boiled *azuki* beans.
4) Stir agaragar into 6 tbsps water and boil for 3 minutes to make paste.
5) Brush sweet potato balls with agaragar paste, place in molds and leave for 30 minutes.

Cal.	Time	Cost
412	C	B

77 · Pancake sandwich
[*Dorayaki* どら焼き]

| INGREDIENTS |

3 eggs (*tamago* 卵)
1 tsp baking powder or baking soda
1⅔ cups flour (*komugiko* 小麦粉)
1 tbsp honey (*hachimitsu* ハチミツ)
80 ml water
⅓ cup *azuki* beans, canned (*yude azuki no kanzume* ゆでアズキの缶詰)
1 tbsp *mirin*
1 cup sugar

1) Sift together flour and baking powder.
2) Beat eggs together with sugar, honey and water. Add to dry ingredients and mix into a batter.
3) Heat a hot plate or skillet to medium heat. Grease hot plate. Pour enough batter onto hot plate to make 10-cm-diameter pancake. When bubbles form, turn over and cook until golden brown. Leave to cool. Mixture makes 16 pancakes.
4) Spread pancake with *azuki* beans and top with another pancake. Continue in this way until you have 8 *dorayaki*.

| NOTE |

• Any jams, custard cream, chocolate cream, or whipped cream can be used as filling.

Appendix

How to cut vegetables:

A) *koguchigiri*—Chop: slim roots such as chives and long onion

B) *wagiri*—Cut into rings: carrot, radish, lotus root, sweet potato, eggplant and cucumber

C) *hangetsu giri*—Cut into rings and halves: carrot and radish

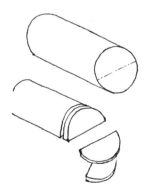

D) *ichōgiri*—Cut into rings and quarters: carrot and radish

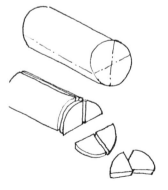

E) *sengiri*—Cut lengthwise and into strips: carrot, radish and cucumber

F) *sasagaki*—Shave into thin slivers: burdock

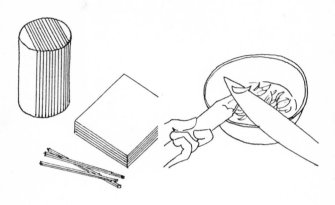

G) *rangiri*—Cut slantwise while rolling carrot: carrot and burdock

H) *nanamegiri*—Cut diagonally in regular manner: long onion